Energise You

Energise You

The Ultimate Stress-Busting Health & Energy Plan

OLIVER GRAY

JAICO PUBLISHING HOUSE

Ahmedabad Bangalore Bhopal Bhubaneswar Chennai
Delhi Hyderabad Kolkata Lucknow Mumbai

Published by Jaico Publishing House
A-2 Jash Chambers, 7-A Sir Phirozshah Mehta Road
Fort, Mumbai - 400 001
jaicopub@jaicobooks.com
www.jaicobooks.com

Original English language edition published by
Crimson Publishing
Mortlake Business Centre
20 Mortlake High Street, London SW14 8JN

ENERGISE YOU
ISBN 978-81-8495-507-1

First Jaico Impression: 2014

Printed by
Jasmine Art Printers Pvt. Ltd.
A-737/3, TTC Ind. Area, Khairne, MIDC
Navi Mumbai - 400 710.

CONTENTS

ABOUT THE AUTHOR

Oliver is living proof that the philosophy behind Energise You works. His passion for health, energy, performance and happiness is infectious. This probably explains why he is both a dynamic, motivating and inspiring speaker and trainer.

Oliver is an ex-professional tennis player and personal trainer. He then went on to manage 14 central London health clubs and qualified as an NLP practitioner before founding energiseYou corporate in 2004. He has coached thousands of top executives and their teams on how to make simple changes to boost their health, energy, performance and happiness, both inside and outside work.

The energiseYou corporate business is the UK's leading expert in health, energy, performance and happiness in the workplace, running workshops in these fields for companies throughout the UK and internationally. The philosophy behind energiseYou is simple: a healthy, energised and high-performing workforce is at the heart of every successful company. This book is based on Oliver's 20 years' experience in the area of energy and the success of the energiseYou corporate business.

ACKNOWLEDGEMENTS

To my amazing team at energiseYou: without you energiseYou would not be such a successful business and this book would never have been created. Also, thank you to all the energiseYou corporate clients; it is through the creation of the energiseYou workshops that this book was born.

Thank you to my Mum, Dad, sisters (Lucy and Sally) for both your support and great feedback on the book. Thank you to Jane for writing your excellent book *Purple Your People*: your achievement inspired me to write this book.

To Vicci, Simon, Noel, Jason, Ben, Jenny, Haley, Dominique, Maeve, Oana, Joanna, Angie, Belinda, Beth, Sam and Andrea for your great feedback on the book.

Finally, special thanks to Ruth for helping to make this book sharp and punchy.

INTRODUCTION

Imagine if you could take a single pill that would give you great health, happiness, all-day energy and success at work.

Well, guess what? This can be achieved. Unfortunately not from a single pill, but by following the habits in this book. By making small, simple changes, you will see your health, happiness, energy and performance skyrocket.

Having coached thousands of people to improve their health, energy and happiness, I have found four common themes, which have driven me to create this book.

1. Very few people have great health, energy and happiness all of the time.
2. Everyone would love to improve their health, energy and happiness.
3. Everyone wants the solution to be quick and simple.
4. Working harder and longer is no longer the answer; working smarter and managing time and energy effectively is the future.

There is a very simple formula for achieving great health, high energy and happiness.

- Consistently do more of the things that positively affect your health, energy and happiness.
- Do less of the things that affect you negatively.

This is where this book comes in. In it you will find all of the habits that give you great health, energy and happiness, as well as the key habits to avoid.

Health, energy and happiness are forever being challenged, so we need to be as consistent as possible with doing the right things. All of the good stuff needs to become natural to us – a habit. In this book you will learn a simple system for creating lifelong healthy habits.

There are seven key elements that impact most on your health, energy and happiness – mind management, nutrition, sleep, exercise, re-energising, computer use and work–life balance – and they are all covered in this book.

Each of these seven chapters contains the following:

- an introduction to the subject
- the benefits of making changes in this area
- the top seven habits that are most important for great health, energy and happiness
- the key habits to avoid
- extra positive habits (after you have implemented the top seven habits, you can start to pick some extra positive ones)
- experiences from individuals who have made these simple habit changes.

The concise approach

You will notice that the information included in the book is concise and to the point – no lengthy explanations with technical jargon as to why you should do this or shouldn't do that. There are four reasons for this approach.

1. Most people are very busy these days and therefore just want to know the right things to do, rather than being told all the details as to why they should or shouldn't do it.
2. I've spent my whole working life reading books that are full of up-to-date research studies and technical explanations, so you don't need to. You can simply be confident in the knowledge that all the information provided in this book does actually work.
3. I have not only incorporated everything in this book into my life, but I have worked with thousands of people to help them to improve their health, energy and happiness, by making the simple habit changes described in this book. You will read about some of their experiences and see how even small habit changes can achieve big results.
4. There are entire books purely focused on one of the seven areas covered here. By including all of them in one book, each chapter contains the key information presented in an easy-to-digest way. In fact, due to the volume of information behind this book, if I was to provide you with an in-depth explanation for each habit, you would be reading a book with over one thousand pages, versus just over one hundred pages.

Even more importantly, don't just take my word for it. Start introducing the habits contained in this book into your life and you will very quickly see and feel the results for yourself.

The 80/20 rule

One important point to make when forming new habits is that the 80/20 rule works; this means: 'don't try to be perfect all the time'. If you can stick to a habit 80% of the time, this will carry you through the 20% of the time when things just don't go to plan. For example, you will have a night when you don't sleep so well, you will have a day when what you eat and drink isn't ideal, you will have a week when you don't exercise as much as you should. But stick to the plan and things will get back on track.

Remember it's your choice all day, everyday

We can choose the good stuff or we can choose the not-so-good stuff. As humans, this is one thing we always have: choices.

In addition to the seven areas in this book, we end with 50 actions that can instantly boost your health, energy and happiness. When you're in need of that extra boost, pick a couple of these actions and they will immediately improve how you feel.

Before you get stuck into the book, why should you even bother aiming for great health, energy and happiness?

Firstly, here are some of the common challenges people often mention.

- ◆ Life feels like an uphill struggle.
- ◆ My energy levels are not good at the moment.

- ◆ I often get a dip in energy in the afternoon.
- ◆ I feel mentally and physically flat.
- ◆ I feel uncomfortable with my weight.
- ◆ I often feel negative about my life situation.
- ◆ I seem to get sick a lot.
- ◆ My work–life balance doesn't feel very balanced.
- ◆ I don't look as healthy as I used.

So here are just a few benefits to working on your health, energy and happiness.

- ✓ Life becomes effortless and enjoyable.
- ✓ You wake up feeling energised, alert and ready to go.
- ✓ You become more successful and perform better in all areas of your life.
- ✓ You achieve your ideal weight.
- ✓ High-energy people are fun to be with; you'll be sure to attract more great people into your life.
- ✓ Your relationships will improve.
- ✓ You'll have healthy, great-looking skin and look years younger.
- ✓ You'll reduce the risk of illness and disease.
- ✓ You'll find it easier to achieve a positive work–life balance.
- ✓ You'll manage your time and your life more effectively.
- ✓ Your mind will be sharper and your memory will improve.

The happiness link

You may still be wondering, 'Where does happiness fit into all of this?' At first glance this book may seem very focused towards health and energy. So, in order to see how this links directly to happiness, let's look at the following questions.

Sleep

- If you have or have ever had sleep problems, does it affect your happiness?
- If you have a bad night's sleep, does it affect your mood and happiness the next day?
- If you have a great night's sleep, do you start the day feeling good?

Nutrition

- If you are over or under the weight you would like to be, how does this make you feel?
- If your health and energy are poor due to bad nutrition, does this affect your happiness?
- When you are looking good, feeling healthy with bags of energy, do you feel happier?

Exercise

- If you never exercise and feel sluggish, do you feel happy?
- If you want to do a charity run with work but can't run even for just five minutes, how do you feel about yourself?
- If you exercise regularly and feel fit, healthy and energised, does this help to make you happier?

Are you seeing a pattern yet?

I'm sure you will have noticed the link between being healthy and energised, and being happy. Ultimately, our happiness is driven by how we manage our mind and our life; good sleep, healthy eating, regular exercise, taking time out to re-energise, being smart with computer use and achieving a good work–life balance all play a key role in not only our health and energy, but also our happiness.

It's all about habits

It really is all about habits and that is the essence of this book.

Let me put it like this: if I were to sit down with someone who is healthy – hardly ever ill – who has great energy all day everyday, and a healthy weight, who performs well in his or her job, who is able to manage pressure and generally seems pretty happy and motivated about life, this person would list a whole load of things they do every day, week and month. Now, if I were to ask this person, 'How do you do all these things?' their answer would be: 'I don't know; I just do them automatically.' Essentially, these things have become habits.

Now, equally, if I were to sit down with someone who is going through a bit of an unhealthy spell in their life, who is over-weight or underweight, stressed, not performing well at work and generally feeling down and negative about life, this person would also list a whole load of things they do every day, week and month. Again, if I were to ask this person, 'How do you do all these things?' their answer would be: 'I don't know; I just do them automatically.'

The healthy, energised, happy person doesn't necessarily do any more or less than the person with poor health, energy and happiness. They just have different habits.

In fact, it is estimated that 95% of everything we do in our lives is habit. Therefore, the key to great health, energy and happiness is to form the habits that help you and to drop the habits that hurt you.

Keep it simple

One thing you will notice when reading people's experiences in this book is that by making just a few simple habit changes they were able to achieve some amazing results.

You will see that I have a 'keep it simple' philosophy throughout the book. This is at the heart of my approach to habit change. Health, energy and happiness don't have to involve hard work; it's all about forming simple, effective habits that create great results. In fact, the more complex the action, the less chance you will make the change and stick to it.

So how do you form a new habit?

Forming a new habit is easier than it sounds.

Start with focusing on three habits for one month. For example, one habit I'm going to suggest you adopt is drinking a 1.5 litre bottle of water each day. By focusing on doing this every day for one month, you will find that, by the end of the month, the following three things will have happened.

1. You'll be experiencing all the great benefits that come from drinking more water and you'll want to continue.

2. You will experience a great sense of satisfaction for having achieved your goal of drinking 1.5 litres of water every day for a month. This will start to improve your natural discipline and willpower which, like everything, is a skill you can learn.
3. You'll find that drinking a 1.5 litre bottle of water is now an automatic habit for you each day.

There is something very important to remember about habits: although 80% of thc hard work is done after one month, and that habit is now formed, you need to maintain that healthy mindset in order to keep the habit in place. Those of you who have ever been really good and exercised three times per week in January and February but then stopped in March will know what I mean!

How many new habits can you form each month?

In my experience of helping thousands of people to form new habits, the magic number is three, so each month pick three habits to focus on.

Do I have to adopt all of the habits in this book?

The quick answer is NO! However, you should aim for the following objectives.

- **Implement the top seven habits.** In order to see a big difference in your health, energy and happiness, aim for as many of the top seven habits in each of the seven areas as you can. Stick to these top seven habits 80% of the time and you'll see great results.

- **Drop the bad habits.** Drop as many of the undesirable habits in each of the seven areas as possible, as these have a negative effect on your health, energy and happiness.
- **Build on the top seven habits.** Once you have implemented the top seven habits, start to work on implementing some of the other positive habits that you feel you can achieve.
- **Three habits per month.** Remember: only focus on forming three new habits per month.

Keeping on track

Here are four things to help you keep on track with your new positive habits.

1. Use this book like a handbook, e.g. keep referring back to the book (in particular, the chapters you know you struggle with) and keep improving.
2. A big factor that really helps a habit stick is what I call the 'feel good' or 'feel bad' factor, i.e. once you know how good a habit makes you feel (e.g. drinking 1.5 litres of water per day), you'll naturally want that 'feel good' hit every day. Equally, if you know how bad you feel after a lunch comprising of coffee, sandwiches and crisps, you'll naturally want to avoid them.
3. Take the online energy check. Taking this check every four months will keep you on track. By simply completing the check, you will be reminded of some of the habits to which you've committed and be inspired to adopt new habits. It's also a great feeling to see your score improve every four months.

4. Once you have taken the energy check, you will automatically receive my free health tips email that I send out on the first of each month. This email, which will really help you stay on track, includes three new habits for you to focus on for the month ahead and reminds you of the importance of positive habits.

About the online energy check

In order to take the energiseYou online energy check, visit www.energiseyou.com. After taking your energy check, you will get a percentage score for each of the seven areas; pick the two areas where you scored lowest and focus on improving them.

HOW TO

USE THIS BOOK

Over the years I've read hundreds of books on the subject of health, energy and happiness. Apart from a few exceptions, all of them have one thing in common: they give you all of the information and expect you to know what to do with it.

Based on the experience gained from energiseYou corporate and the thousands of employees we have coached, both in the UK and internationally, we know that information alone is rarely enough. Yes, about 5% of people will take the information and apply it to create amazing results, but most people need a system to go with all of the information.

As I'm sure you will agree, you can have all the knowledge in the world about health, energy and happiness, but if you don't use that knowledge, you are no different from the person next door who has no knowledge.

Below is a simple system to help you digest the information in the book and convert it into positive change for your life.

Making change a reality

- Read the section on habits in the introduction. This will ensure you understand the importance of habits and how to create new ones.

- Take the online energy check at www.energiseyou.com. You will see your overall score plus your score for each of the seven areas. Look at the area in which you have scored lowest and read the chapter on that area. Then set yourself three habits, from the top seven habits, on which to focus for the month ahead.
- You can retake the energy check as often as you like. Each time you take your check you will be emailed your results and you will also have access to the results from the previous two checks you took. This will allow you to track your progress over time.
- When you feel you need an energy lift, go through the list of 50 actions to boost your health, energy and happiness, and pick two you can do straight away.

1

MIND MANAGEMENT

About mind management

Our mind ultimately controls everything: our health, energy, performance, success and happiness. How we manage our thinking, handle stress, deal with loss and stay positive in a world that can seem to throw so much negativity our way are all challenges that we face.

In my experience of helping people with mind management, this subject often appears, at first glance, not as exciting and tangible as something like nutrition or exercise; thus, it is often viewed as less important. However, mind management is at the heart of everything we do. Crack this, and everything else becomes easy.

Another reason why this subject often doesn't interest people is the association with the thousands of self-help books that are published every year. You, like many others, may see self-help as that fluffy stuff that other people do. ***But***, let me assure you, whether you are a top sports person striving to improve your performance, a top executive wanting to achieve more success or an office worker trying to manage pressure better and improve happiness, this subject is definitely one worth focusing on. As with all the areas in this book, my approach to mind management is simple and practical.

I urge you to try three of the top seven habits for a month, and you will see just how powerful the mind can be.

But first, why do we find it so challenging to stay positive and happy?

The simple truth is that we are bombarded daily with negativity and perceived challenges. I say 'perceived' because often we face situations that we think are major problems, when in reality it is only our perception of them that creates the issue; the situation can be neutral. Here are some examples of how we are being bombarded with negativity.

- **Personal challenges.** These can include health, family, friends, partner, work, home and finances.
- **The negative media.** Wouldn't it be great to have a TV news channel that only reports on positive news? It seems only fair, considering that all the other news channels mainly report on the negative news.
- **Dealing with loss.** This could mean someone dying or a relationship break-up.
- **Our mind** is hardwired to be drawn to what's wrong and potentially dangerous; it's what has kept us alive and evolving for thousands of years.
- **Our focus** is often more on the 5% of our lives that we perceive as bad or wrong rather than the 95% that is good.

The benefits of mind management

- ✓ Creates a strong positive mindset that becomes your natural state of mind.
- ✓ Keep positive and happy even during tough times.
- ✓ Overcome loss quicker, with less suffering.
- ✓ Feel motivated and full of energy.
- ✓ Create the future you desire.
- ✓ Manage stress and pressure better.
- ✓ Stay looking younger for longer.
- ✓ Keep healthy and energised.

TOP 7 Mind Management Habits

The first five of my top seven mind management habits are designed to keep you positive and happy.

❶ *List what you are grateful for*

Each day make a list of all the things that have happened during that day for which you are grateful, and also add anything in your life for which you are generally grateful. Using the notepad or memo section of your mobile phone is a good way to do this, as it means you can write it at any time of the day, wherever you are. There's an example over the page.

Great night's sleep

Enjoyable morning workout

Delicious, healthy breakfast

Feeling happy and energised

Exchanged some nice texts with Mum

Positive meeting with my boss

The sun is shining

❷ *Your life is great; how can it get better?*

Add another page on your notepad, where you can write the seven best things in your life and your top seven goals for the future (below is an example).

My seven best things	My top seven goals for the future
1. My health and energy	1. Keep healthy and energised
2. I feel positive and happy	2. Stay positive and happy
3. I have an amazing family	3. Help my family to be healthy and happy
4. I have great friends	4. Get married and have three children
5. My gorgeous partner	5. Become fluent in Italian
6. My lovely home	6. Spend more time with my friends
7. My job	7. Own a five-bedroom house in a great area

- Every day read these two lists and spend a couple of minutes thinking about them.
- Also, if you have any inspiration to set actions on your goals, write them on your to-do list.

◆ By looking at your goals each day, you will be helping them to become reality. Just ensure you take action when you feel inspired.

❸ *Live in the now*

It is estimated that, for most people, **98% of thoughts are repetitive.** This clearly isn't very productive and can drain a lot of energy. All this continuous thinking tends to be about the past and future, which means we miss the beauty of the present moment. If we don't give the present moment our full attention then we are not giving life our attention. Therefore, this is one of my favourite habits in the whole book.

Live in the now. This habit will help you to live life in the present moment, and achieving this will have the biggest impact on health, energy, happiness and success.

Pick three things you do every day. Each day do these three things with 100% focus, being present in that moment without thought; the Buddhists call this 'mindfulness'.

Here are some examples I've used:

◆ having a shower

◆ eating breakfast

◆ an important project at work

◆ gym workout

◆ reading a child a story.

The key with this practice is to be aware of all your senses and to be totally absorbed in doing. This means your mind is 100% focused on what you are doing rather than thinking.

❹ *List what you love doing and do more of it*

Make a list of all the things that you love to spend your time doing – whatever makes you feel great and fills you with joy. For example:

- getting your hair done
- your favourite food
- spending time with friends and family
- being in the sun
- meditation and yoga
- holidays.

This process alone is a great way to make you feel good, as you will realise just how many things there are in your life that you love. The next part of this process is to set a plan for how you can spend more time each day, week and month doing these things that make you feel great.

❺ *Spend more time with your favourite people*

Make a list of the top five people in your life that you love and who make you feel good. Set yourself a recurring alarm on your phone (I suggest choosing a Monday) to remind you to make contact with them and, if possible, arrange to spend time with some of them. The more time you're in contact with your favourite people the happier you are.

❻ *Positive thinking*

Always talk and think positively about your current circumstances; there's a positive angle to all situations. If you are struggling to think positively then talk to a friend or family member who has an optimistic outlook, as they will help you see the positives in the situation.

❼ *Play to your strengths*

At work and/or outside work, use your natural talents and strengths. Ask yourself the following questions.

- Do I have the opportunity to do what I do best every day?
- Do I love what I do?
- Do I find what I do effortless?
- Can I do what I do consistently to a high standard most of the time?

Mind management habits to avoid

These habits will negatively affect your health, energy and happiness.

- ✗ Thinking, worrying and talking about the past; focus instead on the here and now.
- ✗ Putting off your happiness until the future, as this pattern can become a bad habit. I call this 'the when/then game' (e.g. 'When I have a partner, then I'll be happy'; 'When I get my promotion at work, then I'll be happy'; 'When I get my own property, then I'll be happy'; 'When I earn more money, then I'll be happy'). Remember that happiness can only be found now, because now is all there ever is. Find your happiness in all the great things you have now.
- ✗ Negative talking and thinking – both to yourself, in your mind, and when talking with others.

- ✗ Speaking badly of others.
- ✗ Spending too much time with people who drain your energy.
- ✗ Comparing yourself to others. As all athletes do, focus on improving your personal best.
- ✗ Taking life too seriously – laugh at yourself and situations more.
- ✗ Giving yourself negative labels, such as 'I'm unlucky', 'life is tough', 'I'm bad with money', 'I'll never fall in love and meet the perfect partner'. Eventually, these labels will become your reality.

Extra positive mind management habits

- ✓ Set realistic monthly and six-monthly goals: regular achievements are not only a great energiser but also a key driver in your happiness.
- ✓ Schedule important tasks, meetings or project work at the start of the day, when you have the best mind energy. Schedule emails and admin for the end of the day, when you have less mind energy.
- ✓ Relax and go with the flow of life; take inspired effortless action on your goals as opposed to forced action, which is often driven by fear.
- ✓ Learn the power of deep relaxation for creative thinking; when your mind and body are relaxed, creativity will flow.

- ✓ Work in high intensity intervals of around 1–2 hours and then build in quality recovery time before you go back to work. This could be as simple as a few desk stretches, some breathing exercises or a five-minute walk outside.
- ✓ Manage email traffic rather than letting it manage you by following these four golden rules.

  1. Switch off from work: avoid emails in the evenings and weekends. Also, turn off the auto email push on your Smartphone.
  2. In order to avoid constant interruptions to your focus, turn off audio alerts on your email and phone.
  3. Go through and clear your emails and voicemail at designated times once or twice a day. Manage your colleagues' expectations. You can check your emails throughout the day so that if an urgent email comes in, you can deal with it straight away, but all the others can get cleared together.
  4. When you go through your emails, execute one of these five actions on each one: 1) delete; 2) respond then delete; 3) forward to someone else then delete; 4) unsubscribe if you are on a mailing list then delete; 5) if the email does not need dealing with for a couple of weeks then file it in a follow-up folder, which you can go through and clear once a week.

- ✓ Remember the 80/20 rule: 80% of your results come from 20% of your effort and time. Focus your energy on the things that make the biggest impact – what tasks can be removed from your job/life?

Think about unimportant activities that drain your energy and can be stopped or delegated. How can you spend more time on the things that make a big difference to your work and life?

✓ A project will swell to fill the time you set aside for it. Increase productivity by setting a short deadline for each project. You'll be amazed what can be achieved when you set yourself a challenging schedule.

✓ Improve focus and energy by doing one task at a time. This is the opposite of multitasking (e.g. 4–5pm each day clear your emails).

✓ If you have challenges at work, what conversation can you have with your line manager to bring about positive change?

✓ If you're having negative thoughts, use what I call 'tennis thinking': if a negative thought comes into your mind, create an opposite positive thought to hit back with. Keep the positive thought going until you win, game set and match(e.g. use 'I'm now free to meet the man/woman of my dreams' to beat 'I'm so upset my relationship is over').

✓ Follow this simple system for managing pressure or when you feel like you are overloaded with work.

1. Notice your early warning signs: they are there to alert you to the fact that you have a problem and things are out of balance. Signs include sleep problems, finding it hard to focus, feeling tearful, skin problems, irritability, low energy and feeling run-down.

2. Act promptly; ask yourself, 'What are the three biggest challenges that are causing me a problem?'
3. Set actions to remove, minimise or overcome your challenges. You may not be able to solve everything straight away but as long as you can come up with an action that moves you in the right direction, you're on the right track.
4. Ask yourself, 'How can I improve my health and energy?' As we all know, it's a lot harder to deal with challenging times with poor health and low energy. Great health and energy will give you more resilience when you hit a tough patch.

✓ Think about which people energise you – how can you spend more time with them?

✓ When can you schedule a holiday or a weekend break? Getting away from your normal surroundings re-energises the mind.

✓ Always celebrate your successes, relating to both work and your personal life.

✓ If it's practical, have a pet cat or dog. Coming home to a loved animal is a great way to bring positive energy into your life.

✓ If you have a big challenge, break it down into small manageable actions and tackle one at a time.

✓ Always focus on what you want in life; not what you don't want.

- ✓ Give yourself positive helpful labels, such as 'I'm always lucky', 'I'm always healthy', 'I'm good with money', 'I'm happy'. Eventually, these labels will become your reality.
- ✓ Take some risks in life. Remember that the best rewards in life often involve risk: holding out for an amazing partner, starting your own business, going on holiday on your own to meet new people, buying your perfect home, etc.
- ✓ Make persistence your middle name; everyone who ever achieved anything great in their life had to be persistent.
- ✓ If you are going through a challenging time, remember this great quote: 'This too shall pass.'
- ✓ Release the feel-good chemicals by laughing more – watch a silly film or go to a comedy show.

BEFORE AND AFTER EXPERIENCES

Lucy's experience: switching off the thinking

Being a corporate lawyer, my mind never switches off. I started to see that this non-stop thinking was the cause of my sleep problems and, consequently, my energy problems. But I couldn't seem to stop the thinking. Friends just said, 'Oh you have an overactive mind.' After learning about mindfulness, I decided to pick three things that I do daily where I could be 100% present without thoughts.

So, for a month, my three were: having my morning shower, my morning or lunchtime gym workout and my evening meal with my husband. During these three activities, I became totally absorbed in the moment, as if nothing else mattered in my life. When I was doing this, I didn't think; it was almost like I was too absorbed in the moment to let thoughts in. This daily practice has really helped me to switch off and it's now a skill I can use before sleep and whenever I'm feeling overwhelmed.

Steven's experience: bringing more joy into life

Before I learnt about mind management, my life felt like hard work. It seemed as if I was constantly walking uphill with a heavy rucksack on my back. As you can imagine, I wasn't very happy. My big lesson from mind management was that I needed to bring more joy into my life, so I made a list of all the things I love to spend my time doing. This list ranged from small things, such as a good breakfast or a long morning shower, to bigger things, like playing with my two boys at the weekend and our yearly family holiday. Once I had my list, the following two things happened.

> *Just by making my list, I realised that I actually had a lot to be grateful for – and I was actually already doing a lot of good things on my list.*

> *I made a plan to ensure that I filled more of my days, weeks and months with those little things that made me happier.*

I've made sure that I don't fall back into the same rut by having a recurring monthly alarm on my phone that reminds me to follow this process each month.

Sarah's experience: managing pressure

On and off over the past 10 years I have really suffered with stress at work. After learning about mind management, I realised what my early warning signs are: a feeling of sadness and being irritable.

As soon as I see these signs, I stop, write down my three biggest problems and set actions to sort these issues. This simple process has really helped me to manage my pressure at work and it has given me more resilience to the challenges when they arise.

MIND MANAGEMENT IN A NUTSHELL

Our mind controls so much: our health, energy, happiness, performance and success. Remember that you are the only person who can control your mind, so take control. Become more aware of your mind, and invest time in learning and following the habits in this chapter so that you can get that control back. The rewards will literally change your life.

2 NUTRITION AND WEIGHT LOSS

About nutrition

Whatever we eat or drink will either lead to great health, high energy and our ideal weight or to poor health, poor energy and weight problems.

Think about a car, which needs the right petrol and oil to perform at its best; your body is the same. It needs all the essential nutrients to perform at its optimum. Putting the wrong fuel into your body will result in low energy and eventually poor health.

Especially with nutrition, remember the 80/20 rule: aim to stick to the good habits 80% of the time, leaving 20% of the time to be flexible with life.

Before we go into the nutrition habits, it's essential that you have a basic knowledge about carbohydrates, protein and fats.

Three simple things to know about nutrition

1. **There are three foods groups: carbohydrates, protein and fat.** Every food you eat is either carbohydrate, protein or fat – there is nothing else it can be. Some foods are mainly made up of one of these groups, whereas others contain a combination.

2. **The importance of balancing carbohydrates, protein and fat.** The average person in the UK gets 70%–80% of their calories from carbohydrates, with the remaining 20%–30% coming from an even split of protein and fat.

   I'm sure you've heard the term 'balanced diet'? Well, a key part of maintaining a balanced diet means having a good balance of carbohydrates, protein ***and*** fat in what you eat.

   As everyone is slightly different, there is no exact rule but as a general rule, if you want to achieve good health, energy and the weight you want, you should aim for around 40%–50% of your daily calories from good slow-release carbohydrates, 30%–35% from good protein and 20%–30% from good fats.

   A simple way to work this out is to make each meal/snack just over half good carbohydrates, just under half good protein and ideally include a small amount of good fats.

3. **There are both good and not-so-good carbohydrates, protein and fat.** In order to achieve great health and energy, and to control your weight, you need the 'good' carbohydrates, protein and fats. These are the foods with which to fill your diet. On the other hand, aim to keep the 'not-so-good' carbohydrates, protein and fats to a minimum.

Below is a list of the good and not-so-good carbohydrates, protein and fats.

Good slow-releasing carbohydrates

Aim to get the majority of your carbohydrates from these sources:

vegetables, fruit, oats, brown rice, sweet potato, lentils, beans (kidney beans, butter beans, pinto beans, etc), oatcakes, chickpeas, basmati rice, quinoa, amaranth.

Not-so-good carbohydrates

Aim to keep these to a minimum:

biscuits, crisps, refined foods (like white bread, white pasta, sugary breakfast cereals), chips, chocolate, sweets, rice cakes, croissants, waffles, potatoes, noodles, white rice, fizzy drinks, and drinks high in sugar.

Good protein

Aim to get the majority of your protein from these sources:

chicken, turkey, fish, unsalted nuts and seeds (see a list of nuts and seeds on page 42), Quorn, tofu, lentils, beans, pulses, eggs, quinoa, amaranth, soya protein, low fat natural yogurt, soya yogurt.

Not-so-good protein

Aim to keep these foods to a minimum, as they are high in bad fats:

beef, pork, lamb, duck, processed meats like sausages, ham and reformed chicken, cheese and full-fat dairy products.

Good fats

Aim to get the majority of your fat from these sources:

fish, unsalted nuts, seeds, olive oil, flaxseed oil, sesame oil, eggs, avocados, olives, almond butter.

Not-so-good fats

Aim to keep these to a minimum:

red meat, cheese, biscuits, crisps, chocolate, croissants and pastries, processed meats (meat pies, burgers, chicken nuggets, sausages), chips and fried food.

The benefits of healthy eating and drinking

- ✓ Maintain high energy levels all day, meaning no afternoon dip.
- ✓ Improved mental focus and performance.
- ✓ Maintain a healthy weight (for most people nutrition makes up about 80% of the impact on weight loss, with exercise contributing to around 20% of your success).
- ✓ Improves your immune system so you're less likely to get ill.
- ✓ Reduces your risk of contracting diseases in the future.
- ✓ Gives your eyes, hair, nails and skin a healthy glow.
- ✓ Helps to improve your sleep quality.

TOP 7 Nutrition Habits

❶ *Great digestion*

This is key for great health and energy, so here are the essentials for good digestion.

- Eat slowly, chew your food well and avoid eating on the move or when you are stressed or upset.
- Have your attention on your food when you are eating (i.e. avoid eating while reading, watching TV or in front of your computer).
- Eat breakfast, lunch and dinner at the same times each day.
- Eat until you are no more than 70% full (i.e. avoid feeling full to the max after eating).
- Avoid drinking lots of water with your meal; a glass of water is fine but too much will affect your digestion.
- Make sure your evening meal is light, and give yourself at least three hours between your meal and bedtime.
- Have a healthy, balanced diet by following the nutrition habits below.

❷ *Graze not gorge*

Eat breakfast, lunch and dinner, plus a healthy mid-morning and mid-afternoon snack.

❸ *Eating carbohydrates with protein*

In each meal and snack combine good slow-releasing carbohydrates and good protein foods.

❹ *Good fats are good for you*

Regularly eat foods high in good fats (see page 32).

❺ *Eating your five a day*

Eat five or more portions of fruit and vegetables per day, aiming for as much colour as possible. Remember that if you're trying to lose weight you should focus on increasing your veggies rather than fruit intake, as fruit contains lots of sugar.

❻ *Keeping alcohol to a minimum*

The recommended units of alcohol are 3–4 per day for men and 2–3 for women. For example, a glass of red wine (175ml) is just over two units and a pint of Stella Artois is three units.

If you like alcohol, drink every other day as opposed to everyday, and stick to the recommended units on those days. Also, if you go out for a big drinking session, remember that drinking water throughout the night means you'll drink less alcohol and feel much better the next day.

❼ *We all need water*

Drink 1.5–2 litres of water per day (this can include herbal tea). If you exercise, are bigger than the average person, are in a hot climate or sweating a lot, you will need to drink at least half a litre more. If you're not used to drinking much water, it will take your body about a month to adjust to the increase in liquid, so stick with it. Buy a water bottle online that you can refill each day; look for one that says 'BPA free' (this means that it won't leak plastic).

Nutrition habits to avoid

- ✘ Eating foods that are high in sugar (e.g. biscuits, sweets, cakes and cheap chocolate).
- ✘ Eating refined carbohydrates (e.g. rice cakes, most breakfast cereals, cereal bars, crisps, muffins).
- ✘ Eating white starchy carbohydrates (e.g. white rice, pasta and bread, chips and noodles).
- ✘ Eating bad fats (e.g. red meat, cheese, pastries, crisps, chocolate, croissants, full-fat dairy products, chips and fried food).
- ✘ Eating red meat; you should either cut it out completely or keep it to a minimum (e.g. only once per week).
- ✘ Keep wheat and dairy products to a minimum – and if you do eat wheat, go for wholegrain versions, such as wholegrain bread and pasta.
- ✘ Cut back on the salt you add to food.
- ✘ Adding sugar to food and drinks.
- ✘ Eating a big meal in the evening, especially one consisting of heavy starchy carbohydrates (e.g. bread, pasta, pizza, potatoes, rice, noodles).
- ✘ Eating low-fat processed foods, which are often high in sugar (e.g. low-fat fruit yogurts, cereal bars, cereals and muffins).
- ✘ Eating fried food, especially if it's been overcooked.

- ✗ Eating fast food and takeaways (unless it's healthy fast food, of course).
- ✗ Eating frozen ready meals.
- ✗ Going longer than 4–5 hours without food.
- ✗ Drinking caffeinated drinks, which should at least be kept to a maximum of two per day (green tea is best) and not after 1pm.
- ✗ High sugar drinks (this includes energy drinks, fizzy drinks, fruit juices, smoothies and squash).
- ✗ Buying junk food. If you have biscuits, crisps and sweets, etc in the house you will eat them.

Extra positive nutrition habits

- ✓ There are three daily supplements from which everyone can benefit (see Useful resources for good brands).
    1. A good multivitamin each morning: excellent for overall health and a strong immune system.
    2. A high quality Omega 3 each morning: excellent for a healthy heart, circulation, joints and skin.
    3. 1,000mg of vitamin C each morning: excellent for overall health and a strong immune system.
- ✓ Eat breakfast within 30–60 minutes of waking. This habit plays a key role in setting you up for the day and giving you energy for the morning.

- ✓ Allow yourself your favourite food once a week as a treat. Take the time to sit down and enjoy it, focusing on eating and nothing else.
- ✓ Choose organic options as often as possible. These foods contain fewer chemicals, which in the long term means a healthier you.
- ✓ Aim for 3–4 servings of vegetarian protein foods per week in lunch and dinners (e.g. lentils, beans, pulses, quinoa, amaranth, spinach, nuts and seeds).
- ✓ Aim for lots of colourful vegetables at both lunch and dinner.
- ✓ Eat vegetables raw or lightly steamed.
- ✓ To ensure a healthy and tasty diet, it really does help if you can cook – you don't have to be an amazing cook, just good enough.
- ✓ If you suspect that you might be intolerant to any of the foods you eat, find out by taking a food intolerance test. A good one is the York food intolerance test (visit www.yorktest.com).
- ✓ Be prepared at home and at work with healthy foods (e.g. almonds, almond butter, quinoa, porridge oats, pumpkin seeds, sesame seeds, linseed, oatcakes, fruit, vegetables, olive oil).
- ✓ Have a small plastic food container of unsalted nuts (almonds are best) at work and bring in one or two pieces of fresh fruit. Ten almonds and a piece of fruit is a great mid-morning or mid-afternoon snack that will keep you satisfied and energised for a good 2–3 hours.

✓ Most people's diet tends to be acid forming. Increasing alkaline-forming foods and drinks in your diet keeps you in balance and has big benefits for your health and energy. Here are three of the best habits to stick to.

1. Eat green vegetables at lunch and dinner as often as possible.
2. Eat almonds daily: 10–15 is a good amount as a snack.
3. Drink alkaline water (you will need to buy an alkaline water filter or use alkaline drops).

✓ Buy a juicer and 'juice' at least three times per week.

✓ For super health and super high energy, add some superfoods into your diet. The following are high in antioxidants and are excellent for your overall health and well-being: blueberries, goji berries, chia seeds, blackberries, raspberries, apples, oranges, pecan nuts, walnuts, artichokes, avocado, broccoli, plums, prunes, kiwis, lentils, kidney beans, asparagus, red cabbage and dark chocolate (70% or more cocoa – but remember: have in moderation!).

✓ Do a one-week detox every three months, cutting out red meat, dairy products, wheat, alcohol, caffeine and any food high in sugar.

✓ Learn to read food labels. Here are the main things to look out for.

1. How many grams of fat, carbohydrates (which are sugars) and salt the food has per 100g.

2. Fat (avoid food with more than 6g of saturated fat per 100g), all transfats and hydrogenated fats.
3. Carbohydrates which are sugars (keep to a minimum foods that contain more than 15g of sugar per 100g).
4. Salt (choose foods which have less than 1g of salt per 100g).

- ✓ Control your portion size so that after eating you feel satisfied but not full – a good way to do this is to wait 20 minutes before having seconds or dessert. It takes roughly this long for your body to register that it's full.
- ✓ Whenever you drink coffee or alcohol, also drink water.
- ✓ Add a superfood green drink powder to your water (see Useful resources), which is full of organic greens, such as wheatgrass, barley grass, spinach, peppermint and spearmint. It makes your water taste like peppermint tea and is great for strengthening your immune system and boosting energy.
- ✓ Start sprouting beans and lentils. Sprouting is so simple to do and beans and lentils are at their most nutritious when sprouted. Simply place the beans or lentils in a big glass jar with twice the volume of water as bean or lentil quantity and then leave them there for 8–12 hours. After that, rinse and leave for roughly three days. During the three days, rinse morning and evening. Sprouted beans or lentils are great for a salad or with some fish and vegetables.

✓ Be prepared for breakfast. Have two large plastic food containers at home or work with the following ingredients:

> **container 1:** *¾ porridge oats and ¼ oat-based granola cereal*
>
> **container 2:** *⅓ sesame seeds, ⅓ pumpkin seeds and ⅓ linseed.*

For a perfect high-energy breakfast 70% of your bowl should come from **container 1** and 30% from **container 2**; add to this rice, almond or soya milk, or natural yogurt.

Extra helpful nutrition resources

One of the most important nutrition habits for your energy is eating five small meals per day, each combining the good slow-release carbohydrates and high protein foods.

Below are my favourite examples for breakfast, lunch, dinner, dessert and snacks, all of which combine the good carbohydrates with protein to improve your energy and keep you feeling fuller for longer.

Breakfast

Poached eggs on rye bread

Porridge or granola cereal with seeds and almond milk

Fruit smoothie with blended seeds

Lunch

Chicken, quinoa and avocado salad

Vegetable soup with beans, lentils or tofu

Tuna and bean salad

Any salad that has meat, fish, beans, lentils or tofu

Dinner

Turkey, chicken or fish and vegetable stir-fry

Grilled salmon and steamed vegetables

Grilled rosemary chicken, olive oil and vegetables

Honey, mustard and soya sauce tofu kebabs with vegetables

Desserts

Natural yogurt, strawberries and crushed almonds

Apple crumble, using oats and crushed almonds for the crumble

Porridge oats, seeds and nuts flapjack

Blueberries, crushed dark chocolate and cashew nuts

Snacks

Fresh fruit and nuts

Oatcakes with almond butter spread

Soya yogurt with blueberries and seeds

Deli turkey with rye bread

Hummus, strips of chicken, cucumber and carrots

Homemade flapjacks (made with dates, porridge oats, seeds, nuts and honey)

The best seeds and nuts

These are great sources of healthy protein and good fats:

almonds, soya nuts, cashews, brazils, pecans, walnuts, hazelnuts, macadamia nuts, sunflower seeds, shelled hemp seeds, sesame seeds, linseed, and pumpkin seeds.

Avoid salted and roasted nuts.

As a guide, use a dessert spoonful of seeds and about 10 nuts as a good amount with breakfast or as a snack.

Five healthy food and drink swaps

For breakfast

- ✗ Drop the toast and refined breakfast cereals.
- ✓ Go for porridge or homemade granola cereal with seeds.
- ✓ Alternatively, go for eggs on rye bread.

For your mid-morning or mid-afternoon snacks

- ✗ Drop the refined foods, such as biscuits, crisps, rice cakes and chocolate.
- ✓ Go for a piece of fresh fruit and a small handful of almonds, pecans or cashew nuts.
- ✓ Alternatively, go for two oatcakes with almond or cashew nut butter.

For lunch

- ✗ Drop the sandwiches and crisps.

- ✓ Go for a big salad containing protein (e.g. chicken, fish, beans, lentils) or bring in a portion of last night's healthy dinner.
- ✓ Alternatively, have a big vegetable soup containing protein (e.g. chicken, fish, beans, lentils).

For dinner

- ✗ Drop the heavy starchy carbohydrates, such as bread, pasta, rice and potatoes.
- ✓ Go for a light dinner containing protein (e.g. chicken, fish, beans, lentils or tofu) and lots of colourful vegetables (e.g. a prawn and vegetable curry or grilled chicken kebabs and steamed vegetables).

Drinks

- ✗ Drop the tea, coffee and fizzy/sugary drinks.
- ✓ Go for water and herbal teas.
- ✓ Alternatively, if you find water hard work, make up a 1.5 litre bottle of low sugar fruit squash.

BEFORE AND AFTER EXPERIENCES

Felicity's experience: eating light in the evening

I used to get home and eat a big meal every evening with my husband, which would normally include either pasta, rice, noodles or potatoes. I'd always have a small bowl of cereal in the morning, as I felt guilty about how much I'd eaten the night before. After learning about nutrition, I realised it was my big evening meal that was the main problem. I now have a light evening meal of fish or chicken with lots of colourful vegetables, and I've cut out bread, pasta, rice, noodles and potatoes in the evening. When I wake up in the morning, I want to eat a good breakfast, such as oats, seeds and yogurt. My energy has improved, I sleep better and I've also lost 7lbs in two months.

Julia's experience: combining the good carbohydrates with protein

I'd never heard about combining protein with the good, slow-release carbohydrates, before my diet was very high in carbohydrates and very low in protein. I now make sure that I eat protein with the good carbohydrates in each meal and snack. I've lost 20lbs in six months, my energy has gone through the roof and I feel great – all from one simple habit change.

Graham's experience: beating the afternoon dip

I used to have sandwiches, crisps, a cereal bar and a piece of fruit for lunch, and by 3pm I'd get the dreaded afternoon dip and feel hungry. I would then have a chocolate bar or a few biscuits to keep me going until I got home for my big evening meal. The weight was creeping up, and when I got married, I decided things needed to change.

I now have either a big salad or soup for lunch – always full of protein, such as chicken or beans – and then at about 4pm I'll have a handful of almonds and a piece of fruit to keep me going. I've found that when I get home in the evening, a nice light meal of fish and vegetables is all I need. It's amazing how great my energy is throughout the afternoon and I've gone down from a 36-inch waist to a 32-inch waist in six months.

Gerri's experience: eating healthy and eating regularly

I have such a busy life that I never prioritised my nutrition. I used to drink 4–6 coffees per day and only eat two meals (normally sandwiches at lunch and pasta in the evening), and in between – to keep me going – I'd eat biscuits and sweets. I now eat three healthy meals a day plus a small mid-morning and a mid-afternoon healthy snack. Also, in each meal and snack I combine the good slow-release carbohydrates with protein. I now rarely get sick, my energy is great all day, my skin looks clearer and my focus at work has improved massively.

NUTRITION IN A NUTSHELL

Our health, energy and weight is a reflection of what we eat and drink. Eating and drinking more of the good stuff gives your body all of the nutrients it needs to thrive. Nutrition really is the big one to get right in order to feel healthy and full of energy. Implement the good habits, while dropping some of the bad habits, and you'll be seeing the results very soon.

Nutrition and weight loss

About weight loss

Since so many people have a desire to lose weight, I felt it was important to add a section purely focused on the subject at the end of this chapter. Before we go into the key habits that will ensure you achieve the weight loss you want, here are some observations that I have made over the years.

Weight loss is mainly driven by nutrition not exercise

Success in losing weight is mainly due to nutrition and not exercise. In fact, your success will be about 80% down to what you eat and drink, and about 20% to exercise. Obviously, good nutrition habits coupled with exercise will give you the quickest results.

Keeping it simple helps your results

Nutritionists and personal trainers often make nutrition and weight loss too technical, and if it's too complicated people are less likely to implement the changes.

The media confuses people with information

There is so much diet and nutrition information in the media that it is very easy to end up doing nothing, because you're so confused about what you should do.

The problems with most diets

- Many diets restrict important food groups – and this can be unhealthy.
- Many diets lead to poor energy levels, which amongst other things will affect your ability to exercise and stay happy.
- Most diets are impossible to sustain and this means that, as soon as you can't handle the diet any more, you go back to your old way of eating and quickly go back to your old weight.
- Many diets push you to make big reductions to your calorie intake. This can slow down your metabolism and thus, when you go back to your old way of eating, you may actually end up heavier than before you went on the diet.

The basics

The information provided in this section is not part of a fancy fad diet and doesn't have a fancy name; it is, however:

- **based on how your body actually works.** I'm going to explain the habits that make you put on weight and the habits that will make you lose weight
- **simple to start and easy to maintain** (e.g. these habits will end up being your normal lifestyle). This isn't a quick two-month weight loss programme; it is a lifestyle commitment
- **successful.** I know it works because I've seen thousands of people follow these simple habits and achieve their ideal weight
- **not rocket science.** If you pick up any book from any leading nutritionist, you will find that they nearly all (I say 'nearly all' because I still come across the odd one who thinks he or she has a magic new formula) agree with the habits illustrated in this section. The reason you will find them all in agreement is simply because this is how your body works. One key difference, however, is that the information in this book is very simple, which makes it easier for you to implement the changes and achieve the results.

Please note that for all of these habits there is what I call a 'discipline factor of 1–10' (1 = not doing it at all; 10 = doing it 100% of the time). The weight loss you'll see and the speed with which you'll get the results are dependent on how dedicated you are to these habits. Also, remember that everyone is different and therefore someone may be a 7/10 at sticking to these habits and get amazing results, while another person may need to be a 9/10 in terms of their dedication to achieve the same results.

TOP 7 Weight Loss Habits

❶ *Setting your weight loss goal*

There are three musts when setting a goal.

- Make sure your goal is realistic, stated in the positive and has a deadline date (e.g. I want to be a dress size 12 by 1 December 2013).

  A realistic amount of weight/fat (it really should be called fat loss, as it's fat you want to lose) to lose is around 1lb per week. However, bear in mind that if you are starting to exercise, you may put on a little weight through a small increase in overall muscle. It is therefore more effective to set your goal based on dress size or, for men, waist size.
- Write your goal down (I suggest using your notepad on your phone). Look at your goal daily or weekly to keep focused.
- Tell as many friends and family about your goal as possible, as this is good for support and motivation.

❷ *Follow the top 7 nutrition habits*

Follow the top seven nutrition habits at the start of the chapter. Not only are they essential for great health and energy, but they will also play a key role in helping you lose weight

❸ *Good fats, vitamins and minerals*

Take an Omega 3 fish oil supplement and a good quality multivitamin daily. The latter will help your body to work more efficiently, while the Omega 3 fish oil helps to give your body the good fats, thereby increasing the body's willingness to release fat through exercise.

❹ *Good sleep helps you achieve weight loss*

Prioritise good sleep, as poor sleep can lead to you craving more carbohydrates and caffeine – neither of which are helpful for weight loss. If you're struggling with sleep problems then refer to Chapter 3.

❺ *Managing your stress levels helps weight loss*

Take time out each day to stop and relax and re-energise. This will help to keep your stress levels down. As with poor sleep, too much stress increases the stress hormone cortisol which increases weight gain – particularly around your middle.

❻ *The best exercise for weight loss*

Build activity into your routine, aiming for 3–5 workouts per week and ideally involving interval cardiovascular training and resistance training. Vary your workouts monthly and also walk whenever and wherever possible.

Interval training can be used in any cardiovascular exercise, e.g. running, swimming, cycling, rowing. Here is an example of interval training.

- Run as fast as you can for one minute; then switch to a slow/medium jog for one minute.
- Keep alternating between a minute of fast and a minute of slow/medium pace, for a minimum of 20 minutes.

An example of resistance training can be: using machine weights, free weights, or using your own body weight (e.g. press-ups, squats, lunges, pull-ups).

❼ *Morning movement*

Morning exercise will have you burning more calories than any other time of the day and it also helps to maintain a fast metabolism. If you don't have time for a proper morning workout then make sure you get at least 30 minutes of morning movement, such as a fast 30-minute walk.

Key habits to avoid that lead to weight gain

- ✗ Eating too much food, i.e. eating more calories each day than you are burning off (the amount of calories required is unique to each person). Avoid calorie counting, it's way too complicated and unrealistic to stick to. However, there are three simple things to focus on.

    1. Follow the top seven habits in this weight loss section and avoid the habits listed here.
    2. Use a trial and error system for portion sizes for each meal or snacks, until you feel you are eating the correct amount of food daily to lose or maintain your weight.
    3. Focus on combining the good slow-release carbohydrates with protein.

- ✗ Consuming bad fats, such as animal fat (e.g. red meat), full-fat dairy products (e.g. cheese, cream), biscuits, crisps, chocolate, croissants, chips and fried food.

- ✗ Eating too many carbohydrates. These convert to sugar when they enter your body, and excess sugar is stored as fat. In particular, keep the fast-release carbohydrates to a minimum, e.g. biscuits, crisps, refined cereals, chips, chocolate, sweets, bread, rice cakes, croissants, waffles, potatoes, white pasta, noodles, white rice, fizzy drinks and drinks high in sugar (smoothies, fruit juice, energy drinks).
- ✗ Eating a big evening meal containing the heavy starchy carbohydrates, such as bread, pasta, rice, potatoes and noodles.
- ✗ Things that slow your metabolism down, e.g. a sedentary lifestyle with no exercise, crash diets and leaving long periods between meals.
- ✗ Cutting out the good fats, such as fish, nuts, seeds (a portion is a dessert spoonful of seeds and about 10 nuts as a snack) olive oil, flaxseed oil, sesame oil, avocados and almond butter. Not only are the good fats essential for great health and energy, but if you skip them then your body will be more prone to keeping hold of the fat it does have.

WEIGHT LOSS IN A NUTSHELL

Weight loss can be easier than you think. Stick with the good habits in this section and be disciplined when avoiding the bad habits. Really focus on this for three months, as this will get you off to a good start and you'll get the motivation to carry on. After three months, you'll find you will have formed the right habits to keep the weight off and to lose more if you need to.

3
SLEEP

About sleep

Sleep is truly your foundation for great health, excellent energy and a happy, positive mind. In fact, if you're not sleeping well, you'd find it almost impossible to achieve this, even by putting in place most of the habits in this book.

The subject of sleep has been profoundly important for me over the years. Some years ago, I personally went through a time of very bad sleep problems, caused by cramming too much into my life. If it wasn't for that really challenging year (I can smile about it now, but at the time there were very few smiles on my face) this chapter would not be nearly as thorough as it is. Indeed, there is nothing more valuable than experience, and in this case I've had my fair share!

Sleep facts

Before we go into the sleep habits, here are some useful facts about sleep.

- If you feel you sleep well, you may not have the need to make changes. However, the top seven sleep habits are good practices to put in place, even if you are already a sound sleeper.

- We spend roughly a third of our lives in bed. Good sleep has so many benefits, getting it right means we're on top of a third of our lives. This in turn helps us to achieve great things in the other two thirds. Therefore, making good sleep a priority is key – no matter how hectic your life is.
- Six to eight hours is the average amount of sleep recommended but you may need slightly more or slightly less – everyone is different. The key is good quality and quantity of sleep so that you wake up feeling refreshed and re-energised.
- Some nights you'll have more sleep than others, and some nights you'll have better sleep than others; this is natural.
- With most things in life, the harder you try the more you get. Sleep can be different: the harder you try the less you manage to sleep.
- If you have problems sleeping, you need to fix the cause, whether that's too much stress, a hectic lifestyle, feeling anxious about sleep, back problems, etc. So although sleeping pills may give you a quick fix, they won't address the root of the problem.
- Your body knows how to sleep just like it knows how to heal a wound. So if you're not sleeping well, it's often something you're doing or not doing that's getting in the way of your body's natural ability to sleep.
- If you can remove the things that are getting in the way of your body's natural ability to sleep, your sleep will improve.

- If you're a good sleeper, you may find you need to implement very few of these habits and still sleep well. However, if you're not sleeping well, you'll need to be stricter when putting these sleep habits into place.
- Finally, good sleep is a habit – and not sleeping well can also become a habit. Therefore, if you're not sleeping well it can take time to create a new good sleep habit. How long it takes will depend on how bad your sleep problem is, how long you have had it and your commitment to making changes.

The benefits of good sleep

✓ Helps you to achieve excellent health and energy.

✓ Means you start the day feeling refreshed and re-energised.

✓ Helps to keep you happy and motivated.

✓ Helps you to maintain a healthy weight.

✓ Gives your eyes and skin a healthy glow.

✓ Helps to slow down the ageing process, as sleep helps our cells to repair.

✓ Helps to maintain a strong immune system.

✓ Improves mental focus, concentration and performance.

✓ Helps to improve memory, brain function and problem solving.

✓ Reduces the risk of heart disease, diabetes and depression.

TOP 7 Sleep Habits

❶ *Create a regular routine*

Go to bed at the same time and get up at the same time at least 4–5 days per week. Aim for early to bed, early to rise (e.g. in bed by 10.15pm and up by 6.30am). If you feel you need more sleep, go to bed earlier but still get up at the same time.

❷ *Healthy nutrition*

Follow the top seven nutrition habits for health, energy and happiness. Also, include foods in your diet that are high in tryptophan (an amino acid that promotes sleep), such as almonds, turkey, bananas, spinach, soya products, oats and eggs.

❸ *Exercise*

Exercise for at least 30 minutes per day (this could include fast walking). Morning exercise is best, but if you exercise in the evening you need something more calming, such as light cardio, light resistance work, yoga, Tai Chi or Pilates.

❹ *The perfect sleeping environment*

Keep your bedroom dark, cool (if necessary, leave the window slightly open), clean, clutter-free and quiet (wear soft earplugs if needed).

❺ *Creating positive associations to sleep*

Keep your bed solely for sleep, reading, listening to relaxation music and sex. The mind and body will then create a positive association only between the bed and these things. On the other hand, watching TV or working in bed will create an association with keeping your mind awake in bed and sleep will be a struggle.

❻ *Calming yourself ready for sleep*

Use the evening to calm your mind and body down from the day's activities and stimulation. Relax before sleep by having a warm bath, reading, having a massage from your partner or listening to relaxing music or meditation. Most importantly, wind down 30 minutes before sleep, thus creating a consistent, relaxing pre-bed routine(e.g. tidy your room, brush your teeth, wash your face and read a little).

❼ *Bed, pillow and duvet*

Ensure you have a good bed and pillow and that your duvet is the right tog for the time of year, e.g. light during summer, medium in the spring and autumn, and heavy in winter.

Sleep habits to avoid

- ✗ Drinking caffeine (normal tea, green tea, coffee and energy drinks containing caffeine) after 1pm.
- ✗ Over-stimulating the mind and body late in the evening (e.g. TV, computer use, mobile phone, intense exercise, working late).
- ✗ Looking at your alarm clock throughout the night.
- ✗ Worrying about the future (e.g. 'How bad will I feel tomorrow if I don't sleep tonight?').

- ✗ Talking and thinking about past nights when you have not slept so well. There is nothing you can do about the past, and thinking about past poor sleep doesn't help – in fact, it hinders you by reinforcing the bad habit.
- ✗ Long lie-ins at the weekend; if you feel you need extra sleep on the weekends, go to bed earlier but get up at the same time as normal.
- ✗ A big meal in the evening, such as pasta or curry. Also, avoid refined carbohydrates(e.g. biscuits and sweets).
- ✗ Alcohol. You may fall asleep quicker, but your sleep quality won't be as good, and you will be prone to waking in the night.
- ✗ Smoking. Nicotine is a very powerful stimulant and therefore can affect your ability to fall asleep; also, you may wake up during the night craving nicotine.

Extra positive sleep habits

- ✓ Learn to live your life in the present moment, i.e. being completely absorbed in what you are doing and not lost in thoughts about past or future (Buddhists call this 'mindfulness'). This skill will help to reduce your thinking which, in turn, will help your sleep.
- ✓ If you do talk about how you sleep to friends and family, always speak positively about how well you are sleeping, even if right now that's not the case. Positive affirmations about sleep will help to make it reality.

- ✓ To help you switch off from work. Plan your next day on paper and note any possible challenges along with proposed solutions. Also, set your top three 'must-do' actions for the following day.
- ✓ Learn to love your bedroom and create a positive association with it. Everything about your bedroom should relax you (e.g. choose a colour that you find calming and smells you love) and this space should feel like your own mini retreat.
- ✓ Have soft lighting in your home the hour before you go to bed. Having a dimmer switch in your bedroom is ideal.
- ✓ Back pain can be a common cause of sleep problems so if this is an issue for you, here are my top three solutions.
    1. Follow the top seven computer use habits in Chapter 6.
    2. Do yoga or stretching 3–4 times per week.
    3. Take up the Alexander technique. This teaches you how to identify and prevent harmful postural habits, and you'll learn how to make simple changes to improve the way you use your body in everyday life.
- ✓ If your work requires you to sleep during the daytime, ask your housemates or family members not to disturb you. Keep your phone turned off and also unplug your house phone; investing in some proper black-out blinds will also help.

- ✓ Replace your alarm clock with a wake-up light, which will help you to wake up naturally in the morning. If the light doesn't wake you up, most wake-up lights have an alarm setting of birds singing, which is a lovely, calm way to start your day.
- ✓ Aim to get the maximum natural daylight first thing in the morning; this will help to energise you for the day ahead.
- ✓ As a morning energiser, aim to drink around half a litre of water within two hours of waking and always eat a good breakfast containing slow-release carbohydrates and protein, such as:

  Poached eggs on rye bread
  Porridge or granola cereal with seeds
  Fruit smoothie with blended seeds

- ✓ Aim for 10–20 minutes of deep relaxation or meditation at the end of your working day. For extra help on this, see Chapter 5.
- ✓ If you are struggling to fall asleep, reset a strong sleep cycle with the following three actions.

  1. Get up 30 minutes earlier than normal (also, be strict and get up at the same time at the weekend).
  2. Only go to bed when you are sleepy.
  3. Don't take naps during the day.

  In order to reset a strong sleep cycle, you will need to stick to these three actions for anything between one week and two months.

✓ If you do wake up, use the time to relax and focus on your breathing. Remember that resisting, fighting and getting frustrated about the situation will only feed the problem. Also, remind yourself that the bedroom is a lovely warm, cosy, relaxing place to be, so why would you want to leave?

✓ Notice unhelpful thoughts that pop into your mind and observe them as just thoughts – they are nothing more. See your unhelpful thoughts like clouds passing in the sky.

✓ Sleep happens naturally so don't try to sleep; instead, let go of trying and trust your body's natural ability to sleep.

✓ Use the habits in this chapter for three months without worrying about the results; sleep will naturally improve in its own time.

BEFORE AND AFTER EXPERIENCES

Peter's experience: a relaxing evening = great sleep

Whenever I had an important day, the night before I'd keep getting this same repetitive thought: 'Tonight I really must sleep well because I've got a really important day tomorrow.' The more I thought this the more anxious I got and the worse I slept. I now make sure that the night before a big day I have a relaxing evening and do my 7pm evening meditation/chill-out for 20 minutes. I do still sometimes get that same thought pop into my head, but now it doesn't take over. I simply notice it as just a thought – nothing more – which then passes, losing its power over me.

Sarah's experience: lifestyle changes to improve sleep

My sleep problem started when I was at university studying law, and I've had issues ever since. I would live on coffee to keep me going through the day and all my friends knew about it because I was always talking about my sleep problems. Finally, I decided to make some big changes.

1. *I cut out coffee and all caffeinated drinks after 1pm.*
2. *I made working past 7.30pm the exception rather than the rule.*
3. *On the days when I felt really wired up, I'd get in from work and listen to relaxing classical music for 30 minutes.*
4. *I focused on eating five healthy small meals per day.*
5. *I'd go to bed at the same time and get up at the same time for 4–5 nights a week – normally, at 10.30pm and 6.30am.*
6. *I started to talk positively about sleep, even if I had not slept well the night before. If anyone asked how I was sleeping, I'd say, 'Great!'*

I realised that I had created a bad sleep habit over the years and therefore it was going to take a bit of time to create a new (good) one. Nevertheless, I stuck to my plan and trusted that my sleep would improve.

I'm glad to say that after about two months I started to see a little improvement and after five months I was sleeping really well – just like I had always done before university. It was just a matter of persevering with the new positive habits I had learnt.

Sally's experience: cutting out the stimulants

I used to smoke, drink about six cups of tea or coffee throughout the day and I'd be on my computer or phone until at least 9pm. I always felt tired but also very wired up.

When I started snapping at friends and family for no reason, I knew something had to change so I stopped smoking, cut out caffeine after 1pm and stopped using my computer after 7.30pm; I now spend between 7.30pm and 10.30pm just relaxing. I fall asleep faster now and sleep through the night; also, my energy levels are great and I feel much happier with life.

SLEEP IN A NUTSHELL

Prioritise sleep; the benefits of good sleeping are **big**. Focus on adopting the good sleep habits in this chapter and dropping the habits that are getting in the way of your body's natural ability to sleep; a good night's sleep will soon become your norm.

4

EXERCISE

About exercise

Movement equals energy. So the more we move, the more energised we feel. Equally, the less active our lifestyle, the more sluggish and tired we feel.

As you can see from the statistics below, the average office worker's week is highly inactive. Having completed this calculation with thousands of people, it's amazing to see the results are almost identical for all office workers.

Example of an average office worker's week

- 56 hours: in bed
- 40 hours: at work, e.g. in front of a computer or sitting in meetings
- 7.5 hours: travelling into work by car, or sitting or standing on the train, bus or Tube
- 10 hours: sitting down when eating
- 7 hours: watching TV or reading
- 8.5 hours: socialising with friends (often sitting)

- 14 hours: cooking, washing, brushing teeth, showering and personal admin.

That's a grand total of 143 hours of little or no movement per week. We only have 168 hours in a week, so that's 85% of our week without movement.

It is challenging to make changes to these 143 hours, so it's what we do with the rest of our time that is particularly important.

Three golden rules of exercise

1. **Movement = energy** – aim to fill as much of your life with movement as possible.
2. **Consistency** – as the saying goes, if you don't use it, you lose it. If you exercise 3–4 times per week for three months and then miss a month, most of your health and fitness gains will be lost because you've stopped.
3. **Find exercise that you enjoy** and that fits your lifestyle, this will increase your chance of being a consistent exerciser.

There are three key types of exercise:

1. resistance exercise
2. cardiovascular exercise
3. stretching exercise.

Each of these three gives your body unique benefits. A good exercise programme should ideally incorporate all three elements, in the same workout; they can also be separated into different workouts; however, it is good to also include stretching at the end of all workouts.

The benefits of resistance exercise

This can be with free weights, machine weights or your own body weight.

- ✓ Increases your metabolism, i.e. you burn more calories each day (even when you're sitting still!).
- ✓ Helps you to achieve the weight you want.
- ✓ Builds and/or tones your muscles, improving confidence.
- ✓ Improves your posture.
- ✓ Strengthens your bones, reducing the risk of osteoporosis.
- ✓ Makes everyday activities easier and makes you less prone to back problems and other injuries.

The benefits of cardiovascular exercise

- ✓ Releases endorphins – the feel-good chemicals – so you feel happy.
- ✓ Improves your energy levels and gives you more stamina each day.
- ✓ Improves your overall health, especially that of your heart and lungs.
- ✓ Increases your metabolism (i.e. you burn more calories each day).
- ✓ Strengthens your immune system, so you're less likely to get ill.
- ✓ Reduces the risk of diseases such as cancer and heart disease.
- ✓ Helps you to maintain a healthy weight.

- ✓ Improves quality of sleep.
- ✓ Increases blood flow, which improves the appearance of the skin.

The benefits of stretching exercise

- ✓ Improves your balance, co-ordination and mobility.
- ✓ Reduces muscle tension and helps to prevent injuries.
- ✓ Improves flexibility, mobility and posture.
- ✓ Stimulates blood circulation and improves energy levels.
- ✓ Improves physical performance in sports and general exercise.
- ✓ Helps to relax, re-energise and balance mind and body.

Examples of resistance, cardiovascular and stretching exercise

Resistance exercises

An all-body resistance-based workout could last for as little as 20 minutes and it could be done just twice a week in order to see improvements. That's just 40 minutes per week to get all the great benefits of resistance training – anything more is a bonus. You could try to:

- take a resistance-based exercise class, e.g. body pump
- get a personal trainer to write you a home-based resistance programme or look one up online

- take part in a military fitness class or an outdoor boot camp circuit class
- do a resistance-based exercise DVD
- use resistance bands (when you buy them they come with examples of exercises)
- join a gym and get a resistance programme from a gym instructor or personal trainer.

Cardiovascular exercises

Ideally, a cardiovascular-based workout should be done three times a week. It doesn't need to be for long: 20–30 minutes at a time is a great place to start. That's just 1 hour a week to start seeing the benefits!

You could try:

- cardio-based exercise classes, such as Zumba, body attack, cardio kick-boxing and aerobics
- a cardio-based exercise DVD
- sports that involve cardio, e.g. cycling, swimming, skipping, running, football, netball and power-walking
- looking up a cardio-based fitness programme online, which you can do outside of a gym
- joining a military fitness class or outdoor boot camp circuit class
- joining a gym and get a cardio-based programme from a gym instructor or personal trainer.

Stretching exercises

An all-body stretching workout could last for as little as 10–20 minutes and you could start by doing this twice a week:

that's just 20–40 minutes per week to start seeing great benefits. Stretches can be done throughout a cardiovascular or resistance workout, in-between exercises or at the end of your workout.

You could try:

- going to yoga or Pilates classes, or getting personal yoga or Pilates sessions at home
- a stretching exercise DVD or Wii Fit, or follow a yoga book or DVD
- searching online (there are hundreds of stretching videos to choose from)
- asking a personal trainer or yoga instructor to write you a home-based stretching programme.

One final point to mention is that there are big benefits for your overall health in combining all three elements of exercise in the same workout (e.g. some cardiovascular exercise, some resistance exercise and some stretching). This is also a great use of time and will leave you feeling completely energised.

TOP 7 Exercise Habits

❶ *Walk whenever and wherever possible*

Remember that the average office worker's week is 85% inactive, so walk whenever and wherever possible (e.g. get off the train, bus, or Tube a couple of stops early to give yourself a good 30-minute walk to work three mornings a week, take the stairs at work and always walk up the escalators).

❷ *Find the exercise you love*

Find something active you enjoy that fits your lifestyle and aim to do this 2–3 times per week. The golden rule with exercise is consistency – if you don't like the exercise you have chosen and it doesn't fit your lifestyle, you just won't keep it up.

❸ *Morning exercise is best*

Morning exercise is best for energy and burning calories, and people who exercise in the morning are always more consistent exercisers. Why? Because more things can get in the way of your plans to exercise at lunchtime or in the evenings. So do 20–60 minutes of exercise at least three mornings per week – it doesn't matter what, as long as you're moving.

❹ *A balanced exercise programme*

Aim for a balanced exercise programme, combining resistance, cardiovascular and stretching exercise.

❺ *Having great energy makes exercise easier*

Ensure you sleep well and follow the top seven nutrition habits in Chapter 2. This will ensure you have great energy for exercise; it will also aid your post-exercise recovery and maximise your results.

❻ *Challenge yourself*

Exercise in your **discomfort zone**. This is not your comfort zone (e.g. sitting on a bike reading the newspaper), but nor is it your pain zone (e.g. pushing yourself so hard that it's really painful).

❼ *Motivate yourself with a goal*

Set yourself a health and fitness goal, making it as specific as possible and setting yourself a deadline for achieving it. Share your goal with someone, this will help you to stick to it.

Inactive habits to avoid

- ✗ Sitting at your computer for an hour or longer without movement.
- ✗ Spending longer at your computer than you need to (e.g. going home after a day's work and surfing the net or social media sites).
- ✗ Spending evenings and weekends in front of the TV.
- ✗ Playing computer games.
- ✗ Driving everywhere. Avoid using your car for journeys that you could do in less than 30 minutes by foot. You'll get fitter, save money and help the environment all at the same time!

Extra positive exercise habits

- ✓ Set yourself a realistic target for the amount of exercise you will do per week, and stick to your plan every week. Some days you may feel the urge to do more, which is great – go for it! But you should always aim to achieve at least your minimum weekly target.

✓ Keep good posture in everything you do. In order to help you achieve great posture, the three best things to do are:

1. yoga
2. Alexander technique
3. Pilates.

✓ Every six weeks, change your exercise routine.

✓ Make sure your weekends involve at least two hours of activity. Combining exercise with friends and family is great, e.g. go cycling or walking.

✓ Have a personal training session. Even if you only have one session every six weeks, it's a great way to keep you on track and get you re-focused on your goals.

✓ For maximum calorie burning, implement interval cardiovascular training into your routine by trying the following.

1. Run as fast as you can for one minute, then switch to a low/medium jog for one minute.
2. Keep alternating with a minute fast and a minute slow/medium for a minimum of 20 minutes.

   Interval training can be used in any cardiovascular exercise, e.g. running, swimming, cycling, rowing.

✓ Incorporate one group activity exercise session per week. This could be with a friend, a personal trainer or a bigger group, such as in an exercise class.

✓ Listen to your body. Give yourself enough recovery time to avoid feeling drained and putting your body under too much stress.

- ✓ Take up yoga, Tai Chi or Qigong. All are excellent to balance the mind and body.
- ✓ Wear a pedometer to monitor your daily steps. Aim for at least 10,000 steps daily and then, once you've achieved this, up your goal.
- ✓ Whenever it's a nice day, walk home from work (if you work further than one hour's walk, get the train to a stop that gives you an hour's walk home).

BEFORE AND AFTER EXPERIENCES

Jason's experience: increasing movement in my life

I used to walk 10 minutes to the train station and five minutes to work when I got off the train, but apart from that I did no other exercise. I realised how inactive my life was so I set myself a goal to get off the train two stops early and have a fast 30-minute walk into work three mornings per week. My partner and I have also started cycling together at the weekends. My energy has really improved and, as I was feeling better, I naturally started to eat healthier. Over three months I have lost 5lbs and I feel great.

Alison's experience: cycling to work

I used to take a one-hour bus ride to work every day and my only exercise was a bit of walking at the weekends. I now cycle to work every day, which is actually quicker than the bus. I learnt that interval training burns 3–4 times more calories than continuous pace cardio, so for three mornings a week I cycle as fast as I can for roughly a minute and then medium to slow for a minute, and I just alternate that for my whole cycle ride. In order to make this safe on the road, I just go hard when I see an open stretch of road and I give myself time to recover when I have to slow down for traffic. My energy and fitness have massively increased; I also sleep better and I've lost 7lbs in the past four months. It's amazing how one simple habit change has literally changed my life.

Simon's experience: changes to my exercise routine

I'd been going to the gym 3–4 times a week for the past two years – either doing aerobics classes or cardio – and, although my energy improved, I didn't lose any weight and my shape stayed the same. I decided to make the following three changes.

1. *Having learnt how important what I eat and drink is to weight loss, I started to eat five small meals per day, combining slow-release carbohydrates with protein in each meal.*
2. *I got a resistance training programme designed for me by one of the personal trainers at the gym.*
3. *Every six weeks I change my fitness routine, as I have learnt that my body adapts to the exercises I'm doing.*

Following these three simple changes, I have now lost 10lbs in the past four months, and my body looks much more toned. I can really see a difference in my body shape.

EXERCISE IN A NUTSHELL

Make exercise part of your weekly routine. So much of our life these days is sedentary, which in turn leads to poor energy. Find exercise and activities you enjoy and that fit in with your lifestyle, as this will help you to stick to it – remember the golden rule with exercise is consistency.

RE-ENERGISE 5

About re-energising

In today's non-stop 24/7 digital world we lead incredibly busy lives. This intensity can result in a build-up of stress and toxins, which in turn can affect our health, energy, weight and happiness. In addition to this, it is rare for our minds to ever stop thinking – even when we are sleeping, our mind can be very active.

Stopping, resting and doing nothing is often seen as laziness, and we think that if we're not filling every hour of every day, we must be 'wasting our lives'. In fact, the opposite is true: high quality relaxation re-energises us to perform better, and it improves our health, energy and happiness.

Taking the time to stop and do less really does re-energise you.

The benefits of re-energising

- ✓ Improves happiness.
- ✓ Increases your energy levels.
- ✓ Improves sleep.

- ✓ Helps weight loss.
- ✓ Improves focus and concentration at work.
- ✓ Helps with solving problems and improving creativity.
- ✓ Lowers blood pressure and boosts the immune system.
- ✓ Reduces negative emotions, such as stress, anxiety, fear and anger.
- ✓ Slows down the ageing process.

TOP 7 Re-Energising Habits

❶ *Prioritise sleep*

Make sure you sleep well each night. If you're having challenges with sleep, follow the top seven sleep habits in Chapter 3.

❷ *Deep relaxation and meditation*

Give yourself 20 minutes of 'stop time' per day during which you could sit in a relaxing place in silence, focus on your breathing or listen to some relaxing music (you can find a great selection of relaxation music online). You could also take up Transcendental Meditation (TM) or any form of meditation; this is a simple daily practice that you can learn on a weekend course (search online for a course near you).

❸ *Being in nature*

Nature has a calming effect on our nervous system, whereas city life is very stimulating. Spend some time in the countryside/park/garden or by the sea at least once a week and don't take your phone!

❹ *Re-energising with massage*

Having a full body massage once a month is a great way to relax and re-energise your mind and body.

❺ *Calming and re-energising exercise*

Introduce yoga, Tai Chi or Qigong into your weekly routine and aim for at least one session per week (even better would be to introduce 20 minutes a day of self-practice in the morning). Personally, I can't live without my morning yoga and meditation – it's the best start to the day.

❻ *Your energising hobby*

Take up a hobby in which you can be totally absorbed; it should be one that stops you thinking about anything else when you are pursuing it.

❼ *Quality time with loved ones*

Spend quality time with your loved ones during which you give them your undivided attention.

Re-energising habits to avoid

✗ Working long hours: stick with your set hours as often as possible.

✗ Working evenings and weekends.

✗ Not taking holidays. Even if it's a holiday at home, plan regular short breaks to relax and recover from your busy day-to-day life.

✗ Continuous thinking from the time you wake to when you fall asleep: allow yourself time to switch your mind off.

✗ Working at a high intensity for long periods (e.g. more than four hours without taking a break).

✗ Constantly checking your Smartphone or emails.

Extra positive re-energising habits

✓ Have a bath with scented candles once a week.

✓ Go for a beauty treatment once every three months (e.g. facial, massage, manicure or pedicure – yes, even men can try this one!).

✓ Once a day, close your eyes for one minute (longer if you like), breathe in through your nose and relax as you breathe out through your nose. Keep your focus on the air going in and out through your nose.

✓ Take up gardening in your garden, at an allotment or community garden (you can find your nearest one online).

BEFORE AND AFTER EXPERIENCES

Daniel's experience: deep relaxation on the train

I run my own business and commute into London each day from Surrey, which takes about one hour on the train. As my business is so intense and challenging, I often find that when I get home to my wife and kids, I feel drained. I don't have any energy left to give them quality time. After learning some useful relaxation techniques, I decided to get some relaxation music to listen to on my commute home. I also bought some block-out headphones so that when I'm sitting on the train, I can only hear the relaxation music. It really has been such an amazing discovery and so simple to do. I listen to the music for about 40 minutes on my journey home and by the time I get off the train I feel like a new man. My wife and kids have really noticed a difference.

Steve's experience: learning to meditate

I work in IT and my mind is usually going non-stop. My life in general is very busy; I never seemed to chill out. I used to find that by the time I got home from work in the evening I was so brain-dead that I could often hardly speak to my partner. I decided to book myself onto a weekend meditation course and I now meditate for 20 minutes when I get home from work. I love the experience of deep relaxation and my thinking really slows down during that time. After my meditation, I feel refreshed and re-energised, and my mind feels so clear that I can spend quality time with my partner in the evening – I love it!

Veronica's experience: lifestyle changes to re-energise

I work in recruitment and spend all day in front of a computer. Most evenings when I get home, I'm on my laptop on social networking sites or watching films. My energy hadn't been good for some time and I realised I was spending around 65 hours a week in front of my computer or laptop. So I decided to make the following three habit changes.

1. *I started to go to a yoga class two evenings per week.*
2. *I made a list of all my family members and friends who energise me. I then make sure I have two evenings a week with them.*
3. *I reduced my time on social networking sites to once or twice a week.*

Thanks to these three simple habit changes, my energy has really improved, and I feel so much happier with life. I'm also seeing my friends more often and have made some new ones in my yoga class.

RE-ENERGISING IN A NUTSHELL

Make time each day to do less, recharge and re-energise. In this case, less equals more: energy, health and happiness. Some of the best improvements I have seen in people's energy levels have come from introducing re-energising habits into their daily and weekly routines.

6

COMPUTER USE

About computer use

Why include a chapter on computer use in a book about health, energy and happiness? Well, as I mentioned in the sleep chapter, we spend most of our life in bed (roughly a third) and, believe it or not, the next biggest part of our lives is spent on computers.

Many of us are spending a quarter of our waking lives sitting in front of a computer – whether it's at work or at home (e.g. booking holidays, doing internet banking, shopping and on social media sites, such as Facebook or internet dating).

Remember that movement = energy and therefore all this sitting is not only bad for our energy, but also bad for our bodies. We were not designed to sit in the same position for long periods without moving. So, although computers can't increase our health, energy and happiness, in this chapter you will learn how to stay as healthy as possible despite all those hours spent in front of the computer.

The benefits of working smart with your computer

- ✓ Reduce and prevent back pain and shoulder tension.
- ✓ Improve health, energy and performance.
- ✓ Prevent repetitive strain injury (RSI).
- ✓ Improve focus and productivity.
- ✓ By correcting your posture, you'll look taller and slimmer.

TOP 7 Computer Use Habits

❶ *Perfect posture*

If you work in an office then speak to your HR department or line manager to arrange a workstation assessment. In the meantime, here are the key points to help you maintain good posture when sitting in front of your computer.

1. Sit with your feet flat on the floor, hip-width apart, which allows approximately a 90-degree angle at your knees and hips.
2. Your forearms should be able to rest on the desk with approximately 90 degrees at your elbows.
3. Ensure that your eye line is level with the top of your computer screen.
4. If you use a laptop, make sure you have a laptop dock. Alternatively, place the laptop on some

books to achieve the correct height, and have a separate mouse and keyboard.

❷ *A chair fit for its purpose*

Choose a good chair. Your chair should be adjustable in height and have an adjustable back. It should be able to swivel and have castors to allow it to move.

❸ *Clean and clutter-free desk*

Keep your computer area as clean and clutter-free as possible. Also, make sure you have sufficient space to work.

❹ *Take regular breaks*

Aim to get up and walk around for five minutes every hour. This will get your blood circulating and prevent the muscular tension that can build up from sitting in the same position for too long. Also remember to drink 1.5 litres of water a day; this will ensure that you take breaks from your computer, since you will have to visit the toilet and top up your water bottle.

❺ *Switch off at lunchtime*

Always make sure you take your lunch break away from your desk and, at least three lunchtimes per week, go for a 20-minute walk.

❻ *A balanced body*

Balance your body by alternating the phone and mouse, i.e. one month use the mouse and phone with your left hand and then switch to the right hand for the following month. This can take a couple of days to master but in the long run it will help you to keep balanced, and avoid RSI and tension build-up on one side of your body. If you spend a lot of time on the phone, get a hands-free headset.

❼ *Energising back massage*

Have a monthly energising neck, back and shoulder massage. This is the most enjoyable way to relieve tension and release all of the trapped energy.

Computer use habits to avoid

- ✗ Working for long periods at your computer without taking a break.
- ✗ Using social media every day, e.g. Facebook, Twitter or any other non-essential computer activity.
- ✗ Playing video games every day.
- ✗ Getting into the habit of using your laptop or Smartphone whenever you get a spare minute. Instead, use this time to switch off and relax.

Extra positive computer use habits

- ✓ Make sure your working environment is suitable (e.g. appropriate lighting, temperature and noise levels).
- ✓ Make sure your computer screen is clearly visible (e.g. no flickering, text size clearly visible and no light glare on your screen).
- ✓ Clean your screen, keyboard and mouse at least once a month.

- ✓ Release blocked energy and muscular tension by standing up and stretching your forearms, shoulders, back and chest several times a day. Hold each stretch for at least 30 seconds.
- ✓ Aim to fill as much of your time when you're not at work with movement. This could be a sport, at the gym, walking, cycling or yoga. As long as it's movement, it's helping to balance all that computer use.
- ✓ Keep your energy levels high with healthy snacks, such as fresh fruit with nuts, vegetables (cucumber or carrots) with hummus, oatcakes with almond butter spread and soya yogurt with seeds.

BEFORE AND AFTER EXPERIENCES

Below are experiences of people following a workstation assessment. The key objective is to ensure that the workstation is set up correctly for the individual and to teach correct posture while at the computer.

Jean's experience: changes to my workstation set-up

I was suffering from pain in my wrist, which was constant when I was at work and had started to impact on my daily life. I had lost all strength in my wrist and could no longer carry out simple tasks such as using a kettle. As a result of my workstation assessment, my screen was raised and I started using a mouse mat with a gel pad to put my wrist in a better position. Within a week I could feel an improvement and within a month I was pain-free at work and able to carry out my daily tasks.

Anna's experience: changing my desk and seat position

I suffered with severe pain in my lower back and I had been unable to sit at my computer for any length of time without increasing pain and discomfort. I ended up taking a lot of time off work, over a three-month period, working from home for most of the week. After my workstation assessment, I moved to a new desk which prevents me from having to twist around in order to speak to my manager. I also learnt that it would be better for me to sit at the straight part of the desk instead of around the curve, so this was changed. I am now able to work a full five days in the office each week.

COMPUTER USE IN A NUTSHELL

We spend too long in front of our computers and our bodies are not designed to sit for such long periods in the same position – we are built to move. Keep your home computer use to a minimum and work smarter by following the healthy computer use habits in this chapter. Also, remember to fill as much as possible of your computer-free time with movement, as this will help to balance the inactivity.

7 WORK–LIFE BALANCE

About work–life balance

To open this chapter, here are a few questions for you to think about.

Why should you bother to achieve a good work–life balance?

We only have one life, so let's make it a good one. A good life means being happy and satisfied, and enjoying great health, great relationships (with family, friends and a partner, if you have one), a happy home, hobbies, financial stability – and, of course, being happy at work.

When your life is in balance, this helps you to achieve great health, energy and happiness, which is what we all want, right?

Contrary to what some might think, if you have good work–life balance, you will actually perform better at work. Over the years I have come across thousands of people pushing themselves like crazy with a 60-hour (or more) working week. I always reach the same two conclusions. Firstly, these people are rarely happy with their situation, because they can see how the other areas of their lives are being neglected. Secondly, these people could often work smarter to reduce their weekly working hours and achieve better results in the process. Yes, every now and again you may have a crazy 60-hour week, but this should be the exception rather than the rule.

Why is rotation important?

In the first of the top seven work–life balance habits I suggest that you score your work–life balance every three months by rating how satisfied you are with the key areas of your life: health, family, friends, partner, work, home, hobbies and finances.

So what do I mean by rotation? Don't try to be perfect in all areas all the time; these areas are dynamic and in constant change. Sometimes one or two areas will need to take priority; for example, if you have a baby then family is going to be a big focus for the first 3–6 months, sleep may suffer and time spent on hobbies may need to be reduced. Or you may have a big project to complete at work so for two weeks you are totally consumed by it and you have less time for friends and family.

Why are health and energy important in relation to work–life balance?

I'm sure you would agree that great health and high energy levels will allow you to do more and have better quality time focused on all areas of your life.

Whose responsibility is it to design your balanced life?

The answer is ***you***! If you leave it up to your employer to design your work–life balance, you may not be happy with the results. An employer's main focus is not your work–life balance, as their attention will be concentrated on clients, profit and operational challenges, etc.

So you need to take responsibility. One challenge with this, and I've had this said to me many times, is: 'How can I create a good work–life balance when the company culture is to start work early and finish work late? If I don't play that long hours game, how will I get on in my company?'

Well, this can be a tough one, but I have seen it happen. Here are four strategies I have seen used effectively.

1. Make it clear you will either start early and finish early or start late and finish late.
2. Be known in the company as someone who works hard and smart, but not long hours. This is almost like creating another culture within the company, and if you perform to a high level, others will follow.
3. Achieve amazing results. At the end of the day, who's going to get promoted? Jon who works long hours and achieves average results or Paul who works sensible hours but has the best results? As I said at the start of this chapter, people with a good work–life balance generally achieve better results than those with poor work–life balance.
4. Leave the company and find another one where the culture is more aligned to your values.

Should you measure your work–life balance by days, weeks, months or years?

If you're trying to achieve balance in all the key areas of your life, every day is too short a period to measure. On the other hand, measuring each year is probably too long a period. My general rule is to look back after each three-month period to see if in that time you had a good balance in the key areas of your life. If not, decide what adjustments you can make for the three months ahead.

The benefits of a good work–life balance

- ✓ Improves your health, energy and happiness.
- ✓ Improves your relationship with family and friends.
- ✓ If you have a partner, it improves your relationship with him/her.
- ✓ If you don't have a partner, it will increase your chances of finding one.
- ✓ Improves your performance and enjoyment at work.
- ✓ You will feel happier with your home life.
- ✓ Improves your finances.
- ✓ You will have more time to spend on the hobbies you love.
- ✓ You will feel motivated and full of energy.
- ✓ You will stay looking younger for longer.

TOP 7 Work–Life Balance Habits

❶ *How does your life look?*

Every three months give yourself a score out of 10 for how satisfied you are with these key areas of your life: 10 being perfect and 0 being very dissatisfied.

- **Health.** When scoring health, give yourself an average score for how satisfied you are with your sleep, nutrition, exercise, re-energising, computer use and your mind health.
- **Family.** How satisfied are you with the relationships you have with your family members and the quality time you spend with them?
- **Friends.** How satisfied are you with the relationships you have with your friends and the quality time you spend with them?
- **Partner.** How satisfied are you with the relationship you have with your partner and the quality time you spend with him or her? If you don't have a partner, how satisfied are you with this situation? There may be times when being single feels perfect for you.
- **Work.** How satisfied do you feel about your job? If you don't have one, how satisfied are you with this situation? There may be times when having time out from work is beneficial for you.

- **Home.** How satisfied do you feel with your home and its location?
- **Hobbies.** How satisfied do you feel with your hobbies? Are you spending as much time on them as you would ideally like to?
- **Finances.** How satisfied do you feel with your overall financial situation?

❷ *More energy gives you a better quality of life*

Using this book, focus on improving your health and energy. Great health and energy allow you to achieve more in less time, thus giving you more quality time for the important things in life.

❸ *Making your wish list*

Make a wish list of all the things you'd love to do, achieve or be in your life. Think big and be as creative as possible (think about your health, family, friends, partner, work, hobbies, home and finances). Now set three actions that can move you towards achieving some of the things on your wish list.

❹ *Free up time*

In order to free up more time for the important things in your life, make a list of all the unnecessary things in your life and work that you could stop doing or delegate. My favourite things to reduce or stop include: texts, emails, Facebook and TV.

❺ *Switching off from work*

Create a clear partition between work and non-work by having a cut-off time in the evening when you always stop working. This includes not looking at the emails on your phone.

❻ *Working sensible hours*

Make working evenings and weekends the exception rather than the rule. Also, avoid taking work home with you at the weekends.

❼ *Flexible working*

If appropriate, discuss a flexible working arrangement with your boss that ensures you can still achieve the same – or even better – results.

Work–life balance habits to avoid

- ✗ Trying to be perfect in all areas of your life all the time. Being good enough in some areas of your life some of the time will help you to achieve a consistent healthy balance.
- ✗ Filling every hour of every day. Build in some contingency time, otherwise your life becomes one mad rush.
- ✗ If you manage people, reduce the amount of time spent micromanaging; instead, create clear objectives and clear boundaries for your team.
- ✗ Spending a lot of time on problem-solving issues that your team or colleagues could be solving.
- ✗ Socialising with work colleagues is a great opportunity to get to know them from a different perspective, but make sure you don't spend those occasions talking about work.

Extra positive work–life balance habits

- ✓ Switch off from work in the evenings by 'brain dumping' your day onto paper. This should include any challenges, with their solutions, and your top three must-do actions for the following day.
- ✓ As with the three zones in which you can exercise (your comfort zone, your discomfort zone and your pain zone), learn to work in the right zone. Stretch yourself at work so that you feel motivated, stimulated and challenged but don't push yourself too hard with long, intense hours.
- ✓ Pick some of the working smarter mind management habits – see Chapter 1. Working smarter allows you to achieve more in less time, thereby giving you more time for the other areas of your life.
- ✓ Learn to be flexible. Life is dynamic and always changing, so flexibility will help you to achieve balance and happiness.
- ✓ When you are busy at work, it is easy to forget to organise your leisure time. Make sure you plan things and put them in your diary (e.g. meeting friends and family, your yoga class, weekends away).
- ✓ When you are with work colleagues, friends, family members or your partner, be 100% focused on them.
- ✓ Learn to say ***no*** sometimes. I've often come across people who say yes to everything at work and everything asked of them by friends and family. They end up drained, with little time for themselves and the things they really want to do.

✓ Give your health, family and friends more quality time. Without these magic three, life can become challenging.

✓ If you work from home, create a separate room/ space for work and close the door on it at the end of your day. This will help to create a clear partition between your work and home life.

✓ First thing on Monday morning, plan your work agenda and objectives for the week; this will help to ensure you have a focused and productive week.

BEFORE AND AFTER EXPERIENCES

Vish's experience: scoring my work–life balance

I have my own business and on average I would work a 65-hour week. My business does really well so my finances are healthy. However, over time I started to feel unhappy with life so I booked a coaching session. In the first session the coach got me to score how satisfied I was in each key area of my life. This is how I scored out of 10:

Health: 3 *Work: 9*

Family: 4 *Hobbies: 1*

Friends: 4 *Home: 8*

Partner: 3 *Finances: 9*

It didn't take a genius to see that my life was out of balance. In particular, I was neglecting my health and the relationships with my family, friends and partner. I also had no hobbies, as my work had essentially taken over my life. So the next step was to set actions to change. The coach explained it would be a mistake to try to solve all the problems straight away, so I started by setting three actions to improve my health and three actions to improve my relationship with my partner. To ensure I keep improving, I have a recurring alarm on my phone that goes off on the first day of the month. Each month I score myself in all key areas and set new actions to improve the balance in my life. This simple monthly habit has made such a huge impact on my health and happiness; I'd recommend it to everyone.

Jason's experience: prioritising my health and relationship

I work for a well-known fashion designer. Although I love my job and I am hugely passionate about the brand, I have found that I am a bit obsessed with work, always starting early and finishing late. At the weekend I was either working or too shattered from the long week to do anything. This lifestyle started to create two big problems for me.

1. *My health started to suffer – easy to see why when my diet was made up of cigarettes, coffee and refined carbohydrates. I would never exercise, as I just didn't have the time or energy for it.*
2. *My boyfriend was starting to lose patience with the fact that he would hardly ever see me, and when he did, I didn't exactly have much to give.*

Following a coaching session, I made four simple changes to my lifestyle.

1. *I made working evenings and weekends the exception rather than the rule: my longest day is now 8am to 7pm.*

2. *Three mornings a week I start work at 9.30am and go to the gym before work.*
3. *I stopped smoking and cut down my caffeine drinks from six a day to just two in the morning. I also started to combine the good carbohydrates with protein.*
4. *Since my working hours are now more sensible, I have invested more time in my partner.*

As a result of these four simple changes, my energy improved, my relationship improved and I actually started to enjoy my work even more than before.

Jack's experience: living life to the full

I thought that my life was fairly good but when I scored myself out of 10 for the key areas of my life, I was a four or five in all of them. This made me realise that I wasn't really living life to the full, so I made a wish list of all the things I wanted from life. Some of them seemed pretty out there, but at the time I thought there was no harm in stating what I really wanted. This process made me realise I wasn't putting much time or effort into the things I wanted out of life; I was just plodding along with the same old stuff. I now know that good work–life balance isn't just about having balance in the key areas of life, but it's also about investing time and effort into the things I want from life. So, following this revelation, I set myself three big actions.

1. *I set myself the goal of running the London marathon; the great thing about this goal is it led to so many improvements in my activity levels and my nutrition.*
2. *I bought the Rosetta Stone language system to learn Italian from home.*

3. *I changed my job, to work in an industry I'm passionate about (cars).*

After applying these three simple changes, I feel healthier and much happier with life. I would now rate my health as 8/10, my hobbies as 9/10 (e.g. learning Italian and going on holiday to Italy as often as I can) and my work as 8/10.

WORK–LIFE BALANCE IN A NUTSHELL

We only have one life, so it's best if we make it a great one by achieving satisfaction and balance in health, family, friends, partners, work, hobbies, home and finances. Be clear about what really matters to you in life. Review the key areas regularly, set actions to improve them and always aim to keep a healthy balance.

50 EASY ACTIONS TO BOOST YOUR HEALTH, HAPPINESS AND **ENERGY TODAY**

We all have days when our health feels under par, our energy low and our happiness off our norm. This final section is your 'quick fix' chapter. Many of these 50 actions are good habits to form for life, but they all have one thing in common: they will all have an **instant** impact on your health, energy and happiness.

Pick one of these actions **now** for an instant result.

Energise with nutrition

❶ *Energise your day with regular healthy meals*

Today eat three meals and two snacks, making sure that good healthy protein foods are in every meal. These include chicken, turkey, fish, nuts, seeds, Quorn, tofu, lentils, beans, pulses, eggs, quinoa, amaranth, purple sprouting broccoli, soya protein, low fat yogurt and soya yogurt.

❷ *Super hydration*

Today give your digestive system a break: halve the portion size of each of your meals and drink two litres of bottled water.

❸ *Kick-start your day with a fresh juice*

Here are my three favourite combinations (you'll need a juicer):

- carrot, apple, ginger, lemon and beetroot
- spinach, broccoli, cucumber, celery, ginger and lemon
- carrot, ginger and lemon.

❹ *Treat yourself to a high-energy smoothie*

Here are my three favourite combinations (you'll need a blender):

- granola, pumpkin seeds, fresh mango, blueberries and soya yogurt
- avocado, almond milk, soya yogurt and honey
- banana, mango, granola, sesame seeds, soya yogurt and almond milk.

❺ *Try a superfood breakfast*

- 5 dessert spoons – amaranth pops
- 1 dessert spoon – goji berries and 2 dessert spoons – blueberries
- 1 dessert spoon – chia seeds and 2 dessert spoons – shelled hemp seeds
- 4 pecan halves crushed
- ½ dessert spoon – cacao nibs and ¼ teaspoon – cinnamon powder
- add either rice milk, soya milk or almond milk.

❻ *Make yourself a tasty superfood salad*

Salmon, quinoa, broccoli, spinach, mixed leaf salad, avocado, beetroot, olive oil, pumpkin, linseed, sesame seeds and balsamic vinegar.

❼ *Go on a one-day detox (extend your detox for a week or a month if you can)*

Here are the top seven things to cut out:

- cigarettes
- alcohol
- caffeine
- red meat
- dairy products
- wheat
- foods high in sugar.

❽ *Energise with two snacks a day*

Make sure you have a mid-morning and mid-afternoon snack; this is essential to maintain high energy levels..

High-energy snack options:

- fresh fruit and around 10–15 nuts
- oatcakes with almond butter
- soya yogurt and blueberries with a sprinkle of nut and seed mix

- sliced turkey with oat cakes
- hummus and strips of chicken with cucumber and carrots.

❾ *A day of antioxidants*

For super health and super high energy, have a day full of foods high in antioxidants. Aim to get a variety of some of these foods into your meals and snacks today:

goji berries, blueberries, blackberries, raspberries, apples, oranges, pecan nuts, walnuts, artichokes, chia seeds, avocado, broccoli, lentils, kidney beans, asparagus, red cabbage, dark chocolate 70% cocoa (just a little!).

❿ *Energise your cells with a good quality multivitamin*

First thing in the morning or in the early afternoon, take a good quality multivitamin that contains B vitamins, zinc and magnesium – all are important for energy production in your cells (see Useful resources).

⓫ *Give your digestive system a break*

Your digestive system uses up a lot of energy, so giving it an easy ride for a day will help to give you more energy.

- Have your usual three meals and two snacks per day, but halve the portion size of each one.
- Avoid foods that your body finds hard to digest. These vary according to each individual, but there are some common foods that the body finds hard work: fried food, red meat, spicy food, raw onions, dairy products, wheat products, raw cabbage and beans.

⓬ *Super pick-me-up*

Swap your coffee for a Matcha green tea. Not only is Matcha a great pick-me-up, but it also contains around 130 times more antioxidants than regular green tea (see Useful resources).

⓭ *Superfood energiser: Maca powder*

Maca is a root from Peru and comes in a powder. This superfood gives you an amazing energy boost; add a couple of teaspoons of the powder to a smoothie, soup or high-energy breakfast (see Useful resources).

Relax, re-charge and re-energise

⓮ *Spend an hour listening to your favourite music*

⓯ *Have a bath with essential oils and scented candles*

⓰ *Get into nature*

Go for a long walk, in an old forest or by the sea – these places are very calming and will re-energise you – with a friend, partner or family member. Really try to be aware of all your senses.

⓱ *Early to bed, early to rise*

Re-energise with a great night's sleep. Sleep between 10pm and 1am is your best-quality sleep, so tonight get into bed at 9.30pm and get up at 6am.

18 *Go for a massage*

This will allow you to really lose yourself and relax deeply.

19 *Acupuncture and reflexology*

These treatments have been around for thousands of years, and both have an energising effect by balancing the body. Treat yourself by booking a session today (look online to find your nearest practitioner).

20 *Energise with silence*

Sit in your favourite room on your own, in complete silence, for at least 30 minutes. Do nothing – just sit and enjoy the silence. Focus your attention on how your body feels and your breathing, as opposed to spending this time thinking.

21 *Go for a facial, manicure or pedicure*

These three treatments can be very relaxing. Taking this time out of the stresses of your day to do something for yourself is an instant energiser.

22 *Ten minutes of breathing meditation*

- Sit cross-legged or lie in a comfortable position with your eyes closed.
- Slowly breathe in through your nose and out through your nose, relaxing as you exhale.
- Keep your focus and attention on your breath. When a thought arises, just observe it and then let it float away like a cloud in the sky. Keep your

attention focused on your breath. (Ideally, you should start with 5–10 minutes and over time aim to build up to 15–30 minutes.)

23 *A holiday*

Book a holiday. Once it's booked, you'll get an energy buzz of excitement.

24 *Deep relaxation to alpha music*

Relax to alpha music for 20 minutes a day. This music is specially designed to change your brainwaves to the more relaxed alpha brainwaves and take you into deep relaxation(see Useful resources).

25 *Have a day of avoiding any energy sappers*

Here are some top energy sappers to avoid, as they tend to drain energy from most people: too much TV or computer use, too much caffeine, too much sugar, anything that causes you stress and anybody who drains your energy.

26 *No phone*

For a whole day, keep your phone switched off. You will find it a truly liberating experience.

27 *A cold shower*

For an instant energy hit, take a cold shower – start warm and gradually go colder. It's great for boosting blood circulation and you'll get out feeling full of life.

Energise with movement

28 *Early morning run and yoga in the park*

Get up early and go to the park, for what I call a 40-minute yoga run.

Run as fast as you can for five minutes and then hold a dynamic yoga pose for 60 seconds. Then run as fast as you can for five minutes and then hold a different dynamic yoga pose for 60 seconds. Alternate this run and yoga sequence for 40 minutes, changing the yoga posture each time. In order to learn different yoga postures, either join a yoga class, or buy a yoga book or DVD.

29 *Start the day with 20–60 minutes of yoga*

Either join a yoga class, or buy a yoga mat and yoga book or DVD to teach yourself.

30 *Arrange to go for a workout with a friend*

Exercising with a friend is a great motivator.

31 *Stretch your neck, back and shoulders*

Release the stagnant energy that gets built up in your neck, back and shoulders by stretching them and holding each stretch for 20–40 seconds.

㉜ *Lunchtime walk*

Go for a 30-minute walk at lunchtime – ideally in a park if you have one near you. Become aware of all your senses, as this will help to ensure you don't spend all this time thinking. It's healthy to take breaks from the constant stream of thinking.

Energise with positivity and happiness

㉝ *Re-energise with vitamin D*

If the sun is shining, go and lie in the sun for around 20 minutes (remember to wear sun protection).

㉞ *Have a positive day*

Today, commit to surrounding yourself only with positive people and positive thoughts.

㉟ *Plan something fun for when you get home from work*

Giving yourself something fun and exciting to look forward to is a great energiser. This could be the theatre, a massage, dinner at your favourite restaurant or meeting up with your best friends.

㊱ *Smile and laugh often*

Today, commit to smiling and laughing as often as you can. It's a great energiser, a positivity booster and it's infectious.

37 *Appreciation for life*

Make a list of all the things that have happened today for which you are grateful, and also add anything in your life for which you are generally grateful. Using the notepad in your phone is a good way to do this, as you can do it at any time of the day, wherever you are.

38 *A gift*

Choose three people you love and do something special for them today, such as making them dinner, fixing something for them or buying them a small gift.

39 *A thank you*

Choose three people who are important in your life and say thank you to them today for something they have done for you.

40 *I love you*

Choose three people you love, and tell them you love them and explain to them how much they mean to you.

41 *An act of kindness*

Choose three people and do something to help them; we all have our unique skills and strengths which can be put to good use to help others. Offering your time to help friends, family or a stranger gives a great feel-good buzz.

42 *Go clothes shopping*

Now, not everyone gets energised by clothes shopping, but many do (myself included!). New clothes can be a great energiser.

Re-focus and re-energise

43 *Take action on a big goal*

Take one of your big goals and set yourself three actions that can move you closer towards it. Make sure you execute one of your three actions today. This achievement will spur you on and you'll reach your goal in no time.

44 *Your achievements*

Look back on your life and make a list of all your achievements. Think about the challenges you have overcome and your successes. This is a great way of getting you in a positive, energised frame of mind.

45 *Your top seven goals*

Make a list of your top seven goals for the future. At this stage, don't worry about how you are going to achieve them. Think big and think about what you really want from life. Write your seven goals on a notepad and look at them daily.

46 *Go minimal*

Go into work and spend your first hour de-cluttering your computer, office and workstation. Go super minimal; a clear desk helps to create a clear mind.

47 *Morning de-clutter*

Go to bed one hour earlier than normal and get up one hour earlier than usual. Spend the first hour of your day de-cluttering your home and then take your clutter and old clothes to the charity shop.

48 *Start the day big*

Today, decide what your biggest, most important task of the day is and complete it first, before you do anything else.

49 *Try something new today*

Try something new today, such as a new route to work, a new food, a new type of exercise or any new habit from this book. Variety is a great energiser.

50 *Health, energy and happiness*

Pick three habits from this book that excite you and commit to them for the next month.

USEFUL RESOURCES

The energy check: score your health, energy and happiness

To take the energy check, visit www.energiseyou.com.

Great relaxation and meditation

- A simple and very powerful form of meditation that can be learnt on a weekend course is Transcendental Meditation (TM). Search online for a course near you.
- Relax to alpha music. For a great selection of alpha music, visit www.silenceofmusic.com.

Nutrition resources

All of the nutrition products over the page can be found and purchased online. Some can also be found in some health food shops.

Supplements

- Daily multivitamin: Solgar VM200
- Daily Omega 3 capsules: Eskimo 3
- Daily 1000mg of vitamin C: Biocare Vitamin C 1000

Great foods

- Biona organic amaranth pops (excellent to add to whole porridge oats and seeds as a breakfast cereal)
- Different brands of quinoa, which can be found in most big supermarkets
- Maca powder by Detox Your World (www.detoxyourworld.com)
- Trek wholefood energy bars and Bounce peanut protein balls
- Meridian Natural almond butter whole nut spread

Great liquids

- Vitalife Matcha green tea
- Green drink: AlkaVison GreenShield Greens (this is made up of organic greens, such as wheatgrass and green leafy vegetables made into a powder to add to your water)

Food intolerance test

For a simple and effective food intolerance test, visit www.yorktest.com

FINAL WORDS

We only have one life, so let's make it a healthy, energised and happy one.

Create a life filled with the good habits in this book and aim to drop as many of the bad habits as possible.

Once your life is filled with these great habits, it will become effortless, rich and fulfilling.

Thank you for reading – the rest is up to you…

Keep healthy, energised and happy!

Yours,

Oliver Gray

Follow me on Twitter @Olivergray7

Find me on Facebook www.facebook.com/energiseyou

JAICO PUBLISHING HOUSE

Elevate Your Life. Transform Your World.

ESTABLISHED IN 1946, Jaico Publishing House is home to world-transforming authors such as Sri Sri Paramahansa Yogananda, Osho, The Dalai Lama, Sri Sri Ravi Shankar, Robin Sharma, Deepak Chopra, Jack Canfield, Eknath Easwaran, Devdutt Pattanaik, Khushwant Singh, John Maxwell, Brian Tracy and Stephen Hawking.

Our late founder Mr. Jaman Shah first established Jaico as a book distribution company. Sensing that independence was around the corner, he aptly named his company Jaico ('Jai' means victory in Hindi). In order to service the significant demand for affordable books in a developing nation, Mr. Shah initiated Jaico's own publications. Jaico was India's first publisher of paperback books in the English language.

While self-help, religion and philosophy, mind/body/spirit, and business titles form the cornerstone of our non-fiction list, we publish an exciting range of travel, current affairs, biography, and popular science books as well. Our renewed focus on popular fiction is evident in our new titles by a host of fresh young talent from India and abroad. Jaico's recently established Translations Division translates selected English content into nine regional languages.

Jaico's Higher Education Division (HED) is recognized for its student-friendly textbooks in Business Management and Engineering which are in use countrywide.

In addition to being a publisher and distributor of its own titles, Jaico is a major national distributor of books of leading international and Indian publishers. With its headquarters in Mumbai, Jaico has branches and sales offices in Ahmedabad, Bangalore, Bhopal, Bhubaneswar, Chennai, Delhi, Hyderabad, Kolkata and Lucknow.

SINCE 1946